Praise for Every Conversation Counts

"In a world of missed connections, the gift to listen deeply is one that nourishes both them and you. But it's not actually a gift. It's a skill. Riaz Meghji's book shows you how you can make every conversation count."

MICHAEL BUNGAY STANIER, bestselling author of *The Coaching Habit*

"Riaz Meghji has created an invaluable guide to the core of effective communication—connection. Through the expertise gained from his craft and learnings from those he has interviewed, his perspective is relevant today more than ever to fulfillment, happiness, and success both professionally and personally."

MARK SHAPIRO, president, Toronto Blue Jays

"A thought-provoking perspective on how we can empathetically connect in difficult times, treat each other as equals, and embrace our vulnerability."

TRACY MOORE, TV personality and entrepreneur

"From compassionate curiosity to our urgent need for human connection to build relationships, this book is an invaluable resource to facilitate bold conversations that create breakthrough moments."

DUNCAN WARDLE, founder, iD8 & innov8

"*Every Conversation Counts* is a call to arms for a world that is struggling with loneliness and isolation. It shows readers how to use conversations to create the human connection that is so needed by all of us."

JUDITH HUMPHREY, founder, The Humphrey Group, and author of *Impromptu: Leading in the Moment*

D0036083

"*Every Conversation Counts* is a master class in human connection. As a coach, communication and connections with my team are so important. This book covers some fundamental habits everyone should read and practice."

TRAVIS GREEN, head coach, Vancouver Canucks

"A definitive playbook to make deeper human connections, collaborate effectively, and thrive in the virtual world."

RYAN HOLMES, founder, Hootsuite

"Riaz Meghji provides a compelling read for our times. He speaks not only to the 'what and why,' but also the 'how' in building authentic relationships. His openness is moving and refreshing, making his book, backed up by science, all the more powerful."

MARGARET MCNEIL, CEO, Canuck Place Children's Hospice

"How we change and why is always the result of listening. As Riaz Meghji reveals in this brilliant work, your authentic self and personal growth is not a quest resolved by your adventures, but rather it arrives through marvelous conversations. In a social setting or in solitude, there's always two teachers in the room."

RON MACLEAN, host, *Hockey Night in Canada*

"Riaz Meghji is a master of relationships and what it takes to establish, nurture, and sustain genuine, lifelong connections that have mutual purpose and impact. This is a must-read—it will change you and the trajectory of every current and future relationship you have in your life!"

SAMIR MANJI, CEO, Sandpiper Group

"Timeless and timely. This is critical reading for anyone wanting to create deeper connections in their life."

BRAD KUBOTA, vice president, Western Canada, media sales and client solutions, Rogers Communications

"A thought-provoking read for anyone looking to improve communication skills in business, fundraising, and relationship building."

SANDI TRELIVING, board of directors, CAMH Foundation

JIM TRELIVING, chairman and owner, Boston Pizza International Inc.

"Insightful, illuminating, and invigorating. As a thirty-plus-year leader of multiple businesses, I can tell you that communication has never before been more critical. This book will give you the confidence to connect in any environment and navigate today's new norm of remote setups."

JIM CASE, CEO, Travelers Financial Group

"Mental illness, social anxiety, and loneliness are at epidemic levels. *Every Conversation Counts* is a thought-provoking read that can be the antidote to our social pandemic and the key to better connections, real conversation, and genuine empathy and love that just may change someone's life. I loved it!"

GARY MAURIS, president and cofounder, Dominion Lending Centres

"*Every Conversation Counts* is a compelling read that shares how to combat distracted listening and showcases the value of empathetic leadership. It is packed with practical tips, great research, and personal stories that will help your teams achieve the kind of high-trust culture and relationships needed to win."

JIM REID, CHRO, Rogers Communications

"When working with staff, donors, or the young people who call Covenant House 'home,' this wonderful book's practical tools, and the stories Riaz Meghji shares, are reminders that when we listen with genuine curiosity and love, we can have an impact that lasts for a lifetime—in a world that's a better place for all."

KRISTA THOMPSON, CEO, Covenant House Vancouver

"A valuable guide to how we can find meaningful moments and create authentic connections in uncertain times."

RICK HANSEN, founder, Rick Hansen Foundation

"Riaz Meghji delivers the tools that sales professionals need to connect with clients in an increasingly disconnected world. He is a fresh, new, compelling voice in the world of personal and professional development!"

JOHN PRITCHARD, senior vice president, national sales, Capstone Asset Management

"A deeply researched, comprehensive take on the intersection of social purpose and the human experience. The world has changed forever in 2020, and you're holding the personalized guidebook that will light your way, illuminate your relationships, and rekindle your spirit of belonging."

JORDAN KALLMAN, partner, The Social Concierge

"Making a true connection with your audience is something many aspire to do, but only a few really understand how to do it. Riaz Meghji decided to change the game and has written a compelling book that will enable anyone to make true, meaningful connections with their audiences or in their relationships right away."

CHRISTOPHER IAN BENNETT, president, Casting Workbook, and former creative director, TEDxVancouver

"Riaz Meghji is one of those rare gems who effortlessly connects with people to reveal their truth and vulnerability. And now I'm so inspired by his own vulnerability in this book. These are lessons of humanity, perseverance, and grace that are invaluable to anyone and everyone."

KAITLYN BRISTOWE, TV personality, podcaster, and entrepreneur

EVERY
CONVERSATION
COUNTS

The 5 Habits of Human Connection That Build Extraordinary Relationships

RIAZ MEGHJI

EVERY CONVERSATION COUNTS

PAGE TWO
BOOKS

Dedicated to the memory of a

good man and an incredible father,

Shamsherali Meghji

Cataloguing in publication information
is available from Library and Archives Canada.
ISBN 978-1-989603-72-7 (paperback)
ISBN 978-1-989603-73-4 (ebook)

Page Two
www.pagetwo.com

Edited by Sarah Morgan and Nick Morgan
Proofread by Alison Strobel
Cover and interior design by Peter Cocking
Cover photo by Charles Zuckermann and Zenna Wong
Printed and bound in Canada by Friesens
Distributed in Canada by Raincoast Books
Distributed in the US and internationally by
Publishers Group West, a division of Ingram

21 22 23 24 25   5 4 3 2 1

Meet Riaz online and receive free training at
RiazMeghji.com

CONTENTS

LOOK AT YOU VS. LOOK AT ME

THE PROGRAM director of a local radio station in Vancouver called me into his office for a meeting.

At the age of 22, I was a runner-up in a contest to be the "Sticker Spotter" to surprise and delight listeners around town who sported a station sticker on their bumper. Even though I didn't win, the station gave me a chance to work in promotions. On the one hand, I was thrilled to join the team, because I wanted to get my foot in the media door and ultimately learn how to become an on-air presenter. Mom and Dad, on the other hand, who have always been supportive, were questioning my sanity: defecting from a safe career path in the financial world? Yikes.

This director was an intimidating figure. He was the big boss—everybody scrambled to look busy when he walked into the room. In every interaction, he would briefly acknowledge me with a head nod then just look at me and listen as if he could read my mind. I'm pretty sure he could tell I was terrified. I was so far out of my element; I wasn't even on the same periodic table.

When he called me into his office for an impromptu meeting, I honestly thought I was being let go. That's a common reality in the volatile media business. Instead, he started talking about life and connection.

"Riaz," he said, "if you want to get ahead in this business, the key is understanding the difference between talking to people and talking at them." He championed the notion of staying in the moment in conversations. "Make it about them," he said. "And always remember, 'Look at you' needs to be greater than 'look at me.'" He told me that the efforts we make to learn about people and actively listen to their struggles by feeling their words, not fixing them, are what create relationships that fuel success.

He didn't let me go that day. It turned out he saw some potential in me, and he'd pulled me aside just to give me that advice. He said he believed in me. I was relieved—and grateful that he'd taken the time to talk to me. That conversation taught me the value of giving more than you take.

A year later, I applied for an on-air gig on the station's morning radio show. I was a finalist, but I didn't get the gig. Soon after that, I gave my notice. I felt like I'd done what I could do at the station.

When I told that director, his response was, "Good. Go be on TV. That's where you need to be." He didn't want to get in the way of what he believed I could do. He didn't just talk the talk about listening and making every conversation about the other person. He practiced that, and he proved it in that moment. Instead of focusing on what my departure meant for him and the station, he stayed in the moment with me and focused on my journey.

Of course, I didn't know it at the time, but not getting that radio job was probably one of the best things that ever happened to me in my career. And the perspective that director shared with me in our first impromptu meeting ultimately helped me build a career as a broadcaster and interviewer. That one conversation planted a seed for every conversation I would ever have to mean more.

"Talk to them, not at them" is a gift I've always carried forward. And those words only became more valuable in a time when people began searching for a heightened sense of human connection.

A year that changed everything— except who we are

As I write these words, it's the mid-point of 2020. It's been a disruptive year that will go down in history for a pandemic that made us rethink everything. Words like "quarantine," "new normal," and "social distancing" became part of our everyday vernacular. Systems that were broken were exposed. Unemployment soared. Remote work was a new reality. People protested for racial justice. Unlearning became a top priority. All of this happened while we figured out how to exist in isolation, deprived of our regular rituals of social contact. And we were reminded that human connection isn't an option, it's a necessity.

According to Sebastian Junger, in his book *Tribe: On Homecoming and Belonging*, "The beauty and the tragedy of the modern world is that it eliminates many situations that require people to demonstrate commitment to the collective good."[1] We don't have to work together to raise a barn or bring in the harvest. The design of modern life emphasizes individual convenience, not solidarity.

That's why disaster can often bring us together and create a renewed sense of community. History teaches us that people don't descend into anarchy when disaster strikes. They pull together. They help one another.

But it shouldn't take a disaster to bring us together. As human beings, we urgently need connection all the time, on good days and bad. As many of us discovered during the lockdowns brought on by the pandemic, isolation can literally make us sick. It can shorten our lives.

Why are our relationships so important?

The quality of our relationships is vital for our health, well-being, and, as we learned in 2020, our survival. Healthy relationships help us live longer and manage stress and anxiety. According to a survey by the National Bureau of Economic Research, doubling our group of friends has the same positive impact on our well-being as a 50% increase in income.[2] Family, friends, and positive business relationships all help contribute to a healthier life. Without meaningful human connection, our mental health can be significantly impacted.

If you're wondering about the quality of connections in your own life, it is never too late to focus on cultivating extraordinary relationships. Why make this a priority now?

"We rise to the influence of the company we keep."

This is one of the greatest lessons I have learned from asking questions for a living as a broadcast television host. Over the past two decades I have had the chance to interview thousands of successful leaders, athletes, celebrities, and difference makers while working for brands such as Citytv's *Breakfast Television Vancouver*, MTV Canada, the Toronto International Film Festival, and TEDxVancouver.

For years, I have documented the countless ways our conversations can help build meaningful connections. How we listen. How we react. The unique questions we can ask to learn what isn't being said. How we can speak up when we fear saying the wrong thing. Most importantly, how we can productively disagree in a polarized climate. Relationships are the foundation for productive conversation.

We all struggle to break through the noise and chaos of our always-on, overscheduled lives and forge genuine connections, whether personal or professional. This book is an essential read for sales professionals who need to quickly connect with customers, leaders who need to strengthen their relationships with direct reports in order to deliver results, entrepreneurs who need to build strong networks of supporters to bring their ideas to life, and professionals in any field who need to learn how to network better. But you will also encounter many lessons you can use in your personal life, to connect on a deeper level with friends, family members, partners, and more.

What to expect from this book

Every Conversation Counts tackles a central question of modern life: why are we so connected, and yet so alone? It digs deep into how and why millions of people find themselves more isolated than ever despite the many technologies that are supposed to make us constantly connected. It also examines how the danger of isolation was brought into sharp relief by the coronavirus pandemic. In the following chapters, you will discover the enormous human cost of this pandemic of loneliness. And you'll learn some practical strategies for building stronger connections, both in your personal life and at work.

Drawing from my 17 years of on-camera experience as a broadcaster and interviewer, I will share a simple five-part framework for building extraordinary relationships in our increasingly disconnected world. By combating distractions, getting past awkward small talk, putting aside the pretense of perfection, and having difficult conversations, you will be able to spark real, authentic conversations. It's funny; the ideas may feel familiar, yet you will soon realize how easy it is to forget these basic habits for human connection. The chapters ahead will help you overcome these barriers and give you the skills you need to cultivate trust and loyalty.

We'll begin this conversation in Part One, with an exploration of the unplanned experiment in isolation that the coronavirus lockdowns created. We'll talk about the toll that quarantine took, and about how people responded to isolation by reaching out and finding creative ways to connect. We'll also explore the pandemic of loneliness that was already spreading even before we were all forced to isolate in our homes.

In Part Two, you will learn the five habits that will help you overcome loneliness and build extraordinary relationships. In "Listen without Distraction," we'll discuss how *leading with listening* can help you connect in our always-on, always-distracted world. In "Make Your Small Talk Bigger," we'll discuss how to get past surface-level pleasantries when meeting someone new, by *igniting your curiosity*. In "Put Aside Your Perfect Persona," we'll explore how *removing your mask* and letting yourself be vulnerable can promote deeper connection. In "Be Assertively Empathetic," you'll learn how *assertive empathy* can help you defuse conflicts. And in "Make People Feel Famous," we'll discuss how you can *make people feel famous* through the power of appreciation.

Since we all need to thrive in remote settings, Part Three explores connection in a virtual world. We'll discuss the limitations of digital communication and the risks of remote work, and I'll share some tips for connecting at a distance. The final chapter looks ahead to the future of human connection and asks the question: post-pandemic, what will change about the ways we live, work, and connect?

We all crave connection. We evolved to be social animals. We were never meant to live alone or communicate only in "likes" and retweets. This book explains why so many aspects of our modern lives feel so shallow and unsatisfying—and points a way forward to a better future in which we all express genuine curiosity about the people in our lives, listen with our whole hearts, show up as our authentic selves, and make every conversation count.

PART ONE

AN EXPERIMENT IN ISOLATION

Human connection isn't an option, **it's a necessity**.

THE SOCIAL
PANDEMIC

————

The presence of healthy relationships had already been missing for some time, **thanks to the pandemic before the pandemic: loneliness**.

"THIS WAS a split-second decision."

When NBA commissioner Adam Silver made the bold move to suspend the basketball season in March 2020 after it was discovered Utah Jazz all-star center Rudy Gobert had tested positive for the coronavirus, he not only helped prevent an outbreak in the sports world, he showed what brave leadership looked like by going first.

In hindsight, the decision was a smart one, and was ultimately the catalyst for other professional sports leagues to follow suit to help prevent millions of sports fans gathering and potentially spreading the deadly virus. What's more impressive is that the decision was made before the U.S. government mandated any action. Golden State Warriors head coach Steve Kerr labeled the decision the "tipping point" for society to understand how the virus wasn't an inconvenience, it was an issue with serious consequences.

I was fascinated to learn that relationships were crucial to Silver's decision. He's known for maintaining connections with a wide range of people, and he was able to call on some key experts when it came time to make this momentous decision. Before making the call to suspend the season, he spoke with noted HIV/AIDS researcher David Ho, who was also working on a coronavirus vaccine; Vivek Murthy, the former U.S. Surgeon General under President Obama; and

John DiFiori, the NBA's director of sports medicine, who was in direct contact with the Centers for Disease Control. He then met with owners or representatives of every team to hear their concerns. He had to make his ultimate decision very quickly, when he learned Gobert had tested positive, but if he hadn't spent time talking to trusted experts and stakeholders, he might not have been able to make that split-second call.

When NBA star LeBron James took to social media to tweet his thoughts, he captured the sentiment we were all feeling: "Man we cancelling sporting events, school, office work, etc etc. What we really need to cancel is 2020! Damn it's been a rough 3 months. God bless and stay safe."[1]

A year of disruption

In the early months of 2020, millions of people around the world embarked on an unexpected and uncontrolled experiment in isolation. For many people, stay-at-home orders seemed to come suddenly—one day, schools were closed, and the next day, everything was. Our routines were totally upended overnight.

By late March 2020, one-third of the world's population was under some kind of lockdown order. The total number of people affected, about 2.6 billion, was more than the number of people who were alive during World War II. It's hard to overstate the impact of something so enormous; something that affected so many people in so many different countries at the same time. It became almost a cliché to say that this crisis was "unprecedented," but, well, it was!

Lockdown looked different in different places, of course. Some lockdown orders were enforced by police, and some were more or less voluntary. In some places, parks and public streets were open for people to walk and exercise outside. In others, people had to carry documents proving they were leaving their homes for essential purposes.

Offices were closed overnight, forcing many people to learn how to work from home for the first time while dealing with a steady drumbeat of bad news about the spread of the virus. Schools and day care centers were also closed, leaving working parents struggling to cope with kids who were stuck at home. Some parents were trying to supervise their kids' remote learning while also working from home—and most of them would tell you it's not actually possible to do two full-time jobs at the same time.

Bars, restaurants, gyms, movie theaters, concert venues, and other forms of entertainment and escape were also shut down. Stuck at home, people turned to puzzles and board games. They binge-watched television. Some started craft projects, cleaned out their closets, or learned to bake sourdough bread. Even in the world's biggest cities, the streets were eerily empty as millions of people stayed home to slow the spread of the virus.

Social scientists are only beginning to understand the toll that all this isolation has taken. But some early surveys are proving what many feared: isolation has serious, long-term negative effects. In one survey, 80% of Brits said that working from home had negatively impacted their mental health. Another survey, of Canadians, found that 84% said their mental health had worsened during quarantine. A May 2020 survey of Americans found that only 14% described themselves as "very happy"—the worst results in 50 years. Research in China found that 28% of parents who were quarantined with their kids could be diagnosed with a "trauma-related mental health disorder."[2]

For many this was a realization that human connection was more valuable than they thought. For others, the presence of healthy relationships had already been missing for some time, thanks to the pandemic before the pandemic: loneliness.

What is loneliness?

The neuroscientist John Cacioppo, a pioneering researcher of loneliness, said that if you were to design a human zoo, you'd have to add a note: "Do not house in isolation."[3] According to Cacioppo's work, there's something about loneliness that is antithetical to what humans are meant to be. Humans are defined by our social connections, and when we lack true connection, it can be profoundly damaging.

Loneliness can come in different forms. Vivek Murthy defined several different types of loneliness in his book *Together: The Healing Power of Connection in a Sometimes Lonely World.*[4] Murthy distinguishes five ways to be alone:

- intimate loneliness, or the longing for a close confidant or intimate partner;
- relational loneliness, or the yearning for quality friendships and social companionship;
- collective loneliness, or the hunger for a network or community of people who share your sense of purpose and interests;
- isolation, or the objective physical state of being alone; and
- solitude, or a state of peace, perhaps coming from voluntary isolation, that provides time for self-reflection.

Any form of involuntary isolation can be damaging to physical and mental health. And unfortunately, all four forms of damaging loneliness identified by Murthy have been on the rise in recent years.

In my own life, I've experienced multiple kinds of loneliness. Growing up, I experienced what Murthy would call relational loneliness and collective loneliness—the lack of close friends or a community of people who shared my interests. At the time, of course, I wouldn't have used those words. I just knew I was originally a socially anxious introvert in a world that was set up to reward conformity and extroversion. I was the kid sitting at home while everybody else partied.

Sports were cool, but I was terrible at sports. Teachers would write on my report cards, "Riaz is enthusiastic to learn. He needs to work on his hand-eye coordination." I didn't belong to any clubs or do any after-school activities that might have sparked friendships. I always felt like I had more to offer, but I never managed to find a place where I felt like I fit. I was a hip-hop and R&B fan in a school full of kids who loved the Smashing Pumpkins. I tried to pretend I was into grunge, tried to become a chameleon to fit in, but pretending to be something I wasn't only made me feel more alienated from the people around me.

Forget talking to girls. When I liked somebody, the most I could do was tap another guy on the shoulder and ask him to go tell that girl I said hi. During my high school years, I remember one girl yelling across the hall, "You know you can just say hi yourself!" But I couldn't. My social anxiety ran too deep.

It wasn't until I found the arts in grades 11 and 12 that I really felt like I belonged somewhere. I'd seen my older brother, Zain, thrive in an improv troupe, and I actually switched schools to try to find that kind of community for myself. And it worked: I reinvented myself as a presenter; I found a place to fit in.

But eventually, presenting created its own kinds of loneliness.

When I first got the job on *Breakfast Television Vancouver*, a TV veteran told me, "This is the never-ending show." I soon learned what that meant: I would wake up before 4 a.m. Monday to Friday, I was live for three hours a day, and then I'd regularly host live events and galas for credible causes. When you're in the public eye, you can't have a bad day, or at least can't show it. People want the positivity. In many ways, it would feel like I was always being watched. I was never really able to switch off.

I would see some random tweets from strangers like, "Just rode the elevator with Riaz. He's not as nice as you might think." Everywhere I went, I was being judged. If I took a two-minute elevator ride to quietly think my own thoughts, I was a jerk.

I was lucky enough to go into the morning show job with some longtime friends in my corner—guys I'd met in grade 12, when I'd finally found my high school tribe. But for the 11 years that I was on the air, I was always cautious about meeting new people. I was single and at times would experience the intimate loneliness that comes from not having a partner, but I felt like I couldn't trust people's intentions. Every time I met someone, a voice in my head would be asking: "Do they want to be friends with me, or do they want a 'friendship' because of the media access I can provide?"

Even the day I met Lori, the woman who would become my wife, people were judging me. I'd been asked to audition to host *The Bachelor Canada*, and I needed legal support to pre-negotiate a contract in case I got the gig. Lori's firm was recommended to me. She later told me that when I left their boardroom, one of her colleagues asked, "Do you think he's really that nice, or is that 'TV nice'?"

Luckily, Lori stuck around long enough to answer that question for herself. Funny thing is, I never got the gig, but it turned out Lori was the lawyer for the show, so she couldn't have represented me anyway. Our friendship later turned into something more. Although I didn't get the "final rose," I did find my wife, so I guess you can find true love through *The Bachelor* after all. Today, our son Nico is almost two years old.

Now more than ever I appreciate the role of being a parent, especially after having lost my father suddenly in October 2019. When he passed away in the hospital he was surrounded by so many family members that I think the nursing staff were a little overwhelmed by all the foot traffic. As I paced the hall waiting for his doctors to give us the final word on his fate, I passed room after room of patients living out their final moments alone. No visitors in sight. I couldn't help but think how devastating it would be to depart this world alone.

But loneliness has always carried with it this paradox: millions of us feel it, but we each feel it alone.

The loneliness pandemic

Long before the coronavirus forced millions of us to isolate ourselves (and millions more to shoulder the risk of working jobs that made isolation impossible), loneliness had reached pandemic proportions around the globe.

According to a 2018 report by the Kaiser Family Foundation, 22% of U.S. adults always or often feel lonely or isolated. In another 2018 study, by the AARP, one-third of Americans over 45 said they were lonely. A Cigna survey found that one-fifth of Americans never or rarely felt close to anyone else. And the problem wasn't limited to America: one out of every four Australian adults and one in five Canadians identify as being lonely. After widespread concern in the United Kingdom, they appointed a Minister for Loneliness in 2018. Hundreds of thousands of U.K. seniors spoke to family or friends less than once a week. Over a million adults in Japan ventured out infrequently enough to be classified as recluses (what the Japanese call *hikikomori*, which literally means "pulling inward").[5]

And all those surveys were taken before coronavirus. There's no doubt in my mind that the coronavirus crisis will end up driving millions of people even deeper into loneliness and isolation.

Of course, people have experienced loneliness since people have been people. But our experience of loneliness is inevitably colored by the culture and times that we live in: is solitude valued or viewed with suspicion? Do most people live with extended family? Do we know our neighbors? The answers to these questions vary from place to place and have changed over the years—and they have an enormous impact on *how* we experience loneliness and what we make it mean.

The very word "loneliness" didn't come into the English language until the 16th century, as one of the 1,700 words invented by Shakespeare. "I go alone," Coriolanus says in the tragedy that bears his name, "Like to a lonely dragon, that his fen / Makes fear'd and talk'd of more than seen."[6] He's just been banished from Rome, and he's trying to reassure his mother that he'll be fine, but this striking image of a dragon retreating to a lonesome swamp, so feared by the populace that nobody will even approach him, sort of undercuts his point. "Don't worry about me, I'll be fine, just like a fearsome, hideous dragon that everyone hates!" Not very convincing.

Loneliness has always carried with it this paradox: millions of us feel it, **but we each feel it alone**.

Prior to Shakespeare's time, people would have used the word "oneliness" to describe the state of being alone. This was basically a positive word, more like "solitude" than "loneliness." Being alone was seen as giving a person time to think and an opportunity to draw closer to God. After all, for most of history, simply surviving has been too labor-intensive for most people to do alone. In a world where most people lived crowded into small homes with large families, where both work and play were typically communal activities, it's no wonder that people idealized the state of solitude.

Loneliness is different. Solitude is something you choose, like Thoreau choosing to go live at Walden Pond; loneliness is something that happens to you. According to the psychologist Dr. Ami Rokach, loneliness happens when there's a mismatch between what we expect our social experience to be and what it actually is.[7] We're not truly lonely unless we think we should be with other people.

Loneliness is more common today than ever before. In 1960, only 13% of American households were single individuals.[8] Today, 28% of households consist of one person living alone. Of course, some people choose to live alone, and enjoy their solitude. But many of those single-person households represent people who would prefer to be living with a partner or friend.

There is something about modern life that isolates us. The seminal book *Bowling Alone*, by Robert Putnam, published in 2000, identified the trend: even 20 years ago, Americans belonged to fewer organizations, socialized less with friends and family, even joined bowling leagues less often than their parents had. And in many ways, our isolation has only intensified since then.

We are more isolated in every aspect of our lives. More of us live alone. Fewer of us belong to labor unions at work—in

2019, just 10% of Americans belonged to a union. Unions represented twice as many workers in 1983.[9] And fewer of us belong to religious communities. According to the Pew Research Center, the number of Americans who don't identify with any religion has grown from 17% in 2009 to 26% in 2019.[10] Today, Americans who say they only attend religious services occasionally, or never go at all, outnumber those who go at least once a month. Just 10 years ago, the reverse was true.

Why are we so much more alone than we used to be? The structure of our economy probably has a lot to do with it. Agricultural work is communal by nature. The industrial revolution, and the shift of populations into cities, began a very long-term trend toward smaller family sizes and smaller households.

More recently, over the past 40 years, the average person's wages basically haven't increased at all (after accounting for inflation).[11] The cost of living has gone up, but earnings haven't. In the 1950s and '60s, it was possible for many people to support a family on one adult's income. Today, most households need two working adults to support a family, and millions of families are still just one missed paycheck away from disaster. That kind of intense, unrelenting financial anxiety doesn't leave a lot of free time or mental energy for volunteering, joining clubs, or even having friends over for dinner.

Who suffers most?

Unfortunately, the pain of loneliness is all too common for seniors. According to a survey by the University of Michigan, 34% of older adults feel they lack companionship at least some of the time, and 27% feel isolated. One in four say they have contact with friends or family they don't live with less than once a week. And these problems are only likely to deepen over time, as the baby boom generation ages. More Baby Boomers have never had kids, and more of them are divorced, than previous generations, which leaves them more likely to live alone and less likely to have family to rely on as caregivers, according to the AARP.[12]

There are a lot of factors that can leave a person more vulnerable to loneliness as they age. Loss of a spouse can lead to isolation, of course. Divorce or childlessness can do the same. LGBTQ seniors tend to be more vulnerable, because for our current generation of elders, LGBTQ folks are more likely to be childless or estranged from family than their straight, cisgender peers.[13] Discrimination can also lead to isolation: only half of LGBTQ seniors in long-term care are out. If you can't be open about who you are, you're going to feel isolated even in a crowd. Poverty can deepen isolation, too. If you don't have reliable transportation, for example, you can't easily join group activities or visit family and friends.

Older people aren't the only ones who are more vulnerable to isolation. People living far away from their families are at risk, too. According to the United Nations, 272 million people were living outside of their home countries in 2019.[14] Loneliness is a huge challenge for migrants, refugees, and immigrants. Not only are you living far from extended family, but you're starting from scratch building a new social network—often across a language barrier. Cultural norms are different from what you're used to. Isolation is an enormous challenge in those circumstances.

In fact, even though loneliness for seniors is a real crisis, the loneliest generation right now is actually one of the youngest: Generation Z.[15] In some ways, it's no surprise. After all, young people who are 18 to 22 right now are growing up in smaller families, raised by parents who are part of all the trends we've already talked about: they're less likely to be part of a religious community, less likely to know their neighbors, less likely to socialize with coworkers. Kids learn from their parents, and kids today are learning from parents who are more and more likely to just go to work and come home, day after day, without much time to socialize.

Expectations probably play a role, too. In popular culture, high school and college are still all about dating, partying, and hanging out with friends. If you're sitting at home watching Netflix, but you think *everyone else* is out having fun, you're much more likely to feel lonely than you would if you knew just how normal you were.

The elephant in the smartphone

Which brings us to technology. Have social media, streaming TV, and other modern conveniences turned us all into hermits? Or is it simply a coincidence that loneliness went pandemic in the age of Facebook?

Technology was supposed to bring us all closer together. And it's true that being able to reach out over FaceTime or trade jokes on Twitter has been a real comfort for those of us socially isolating during the coronavirus pandemic. But the impact of social media is a lot more complicated than that. Sometimes technology does seem like a force for good. On the one hand, using Facebook, Skype, and other social technology can decrease loneliness among older adults.[16] On the other hand, for younger people, studies show that spending *less* time on social media can decrease loneliness.

So which is it? Does social media connect us, or drive us further apart? The answer may lie in *how* we use technology.

Technology can be
a powerful tool for
connection, but it can
also be **an equally
powerful tool for
destroying connection**.

For example, one long-term study of Facebook users found that people who did things like comment on a friend's post, or got comments or likes, felt less lonely.[17] But when people simply scrolled through other people's posts, or broadcast their feelings in a status update, they felt *more* lonely. In other words, if we use technology to legitimately connect with another person we know, to strengthen an existing relationship, it helps. We feel that connection. But if we just use it to shout our thoughts into the void, or passively eavesdrop on other people's lives, we end up feeling more isolated.

Even worse, some people use their smartphones to avoid talking to the people right in front of them. "Phubbing," or snubbing a live person in favor of a phone, is a pervasive problem. We all have that friend (or a few friends) who simply can't stop looking at their phone. Let's just hope it's not your partner: one survey, taken in 2015, found that 46% of people said their partners had "phubbed" them.[18] Not surprisingly, relationships where one partner can't put down their phone tend to be less satisfying, and involve more fights. Technology can be a powerful tool for connection, but it can also be an equally powerful tool for *destroying* connection.

Again, expectations seem crucial. Passively scrolling through Instagram without commenting or really connecting with anyone is only going to make you feel like everyone else is out having fun; taking great vacations; eating brunch; or going for hikes with their attractive partners, cute kids, and photogenic dogs—while you're sitting at home staring at your phone. Sitting down to dinner with a partner who won't stop looking at their phone is only going to make you feel more miserable when you compare yourselves to the ideal, connected couple you feel you should be. That contrast, that feeling that we *should* be connecting but we're not, is poison to us. And looking at pictures of other people's good times is a perfect way to create that toxic mismatch.

According to the late John Cacioppo, arguably the world expert on loneliness, the impact of technology is even simpler. If you use technology to create more face-to-face connections, you'll be less lonely. If you use it to substitute for face-to-face conversation, you'll be more lonely. There is no substitute for in-person connection. We need it. Technology can be a tool to create it—or a crutch that lets us avoid it.

Perhaps that's why, despite our urgent desire to connect during the coronavirus pandemic, so many of us started to suffer from "Zoom fatigue."[19] We'll dig deeper into this later in the book but for now I'll just say that video calls create a feeling of dissonance in our unconscious minds—the person we're talking to is both there and not there. We're working harder to pick up on all those nonverbal cues that we process so effortlessly when we're face-to-face. Plus, the format of the technology can create a feeling that you're performing, not just chatting. If you can see your own face, you're always thinking about how you look.

But ultimately, the real problem is that we all know, instinctively, what Cacioppo's years of research taught him: we need in-person contact. There's no substitute for it. Talking to someone you love over video chat is the best you can do when you're not able to be together physically. But it's not enough. It will never feel like enough. The coronavirus forced millions of us to try to substitute technological connection for the real thing, and we all knew down to our bones that it wasn't the same.

THE SOCIAL PANDEMIC **29**

Social animals

Why? After all, snow leopards thrive in majestic solitude. Why is it so hard for us to be alone?

Well, we're not snow leopards. We're descended from monkeys, who began to form social groups as much as 52 million years ago. Gathering into groups gave monkeys an advantage when it came to fighting off predators. Watch a *Planet Earth* documentary today, and you'll see monkeys living, eating, and sleeping in groups—warning each other of approaching dangers, helping each other find food, and raiding rival bands together.

We tend to assume that it's our big brains that put us humans at the top of the global food chain. But in fact, our ability to bond with other people may be our key evolutionary advantage. If you had to face off against a snow leopard, a bear, or an alligator by yourself... let's just say I wouldn't bet on you. But given the ability to work with a few other people— or benefit from technologies created by people working together in groups—suddenly, the odds are in your favor.

Actually, some research suggests that we developed our big brains *because* we organized ourselves into big social groups. According to the anthropologist Robin Dunbar, you can predict an animal's brain size by looking at the size of its social groups.[20] The first big-brained hominids, our distant ancestors, were also the first hominids to hunt cooperatively, live together in large groups, and bury their dead. According to this theory, bonding with other people is literally *what our brains are for*.

Nature is clever. Things that tend to lead to the survival of the species tend to feel good. And for humans, that includes social connection. According to Dr. Steve Cole, a researcher at the University of California, connection decreases our physical stress response. The drive to connect is wired into us so deeply that it is literally the first thing our brains try to do, the second we're not doing anything else. A study by Dr. Matthew Lieberman, a neuroscientist at UCLA, found that the moment we stop doing a non-social task, like thinking through a math problem, our brains' social pathways light up. "Evolution has placed a bet," Lieberman has said, "that the best thing for our brain to do in any spare moment is to get ready to see the world socially."[21]

From the moment we're born, we are designed to be social. Researchers at Stanford found that a four-month-old infant has nearly the same ability to visually process a face as an adult does.[22] Visual processing of objects lags far behind. We come into the world fascinated by faces.

So what happens to a social animal in isolation? At the extreme, total isolation breaks people down mentally. In 1951, researchers at McGill University wanted to study the effects of isolation and sensory deprivation. They tried to pay grad students to stay in a small room, alone, wearing goggles and earphones and gloves. Nobody lasted more than a week. Several of the students started to hallucinate.

Prisoners in solitary confinement can see and hear, but they can't interact with other people. And that deprivation is incredibly damaging. According to psychiatrist Stuart Grassian, about one in three prisoners in solitary confinement become either psychotic or suicidal. Many develop panic attacks, obsessions, difficulty thinking and concentrating, even hallucinations. Another researcher found that people who'd been kept in solitary confinement eventually lost the ability to interact with other people. Even given the opportunity to come out, they'd choose to stay in their cells, alone.[23]

Obviously, solitary confinement is an extreme case. But even more ordinary forms of loneliness take an enormous toll on us, physically and emotionally. Multiple studies have found that, in our brains, the social pain of loneliness looks just like the physical pain of hunger, thirst, or even a literal wound. And, to our bodies, loneliness essentially *is* a wound. Isolation can kill.

Researcher Julianne Holt-Lunstad analyzed multiple studies from around the world to determine that people with strong social ties are half as likely to die prematurely as people whose relationships are weaker.[24] The effect of isolation is as damaging to the body as smoking 15 cigarettes a day. Loneliness is worse for you, health-wise, than obesity, excess drinking, or failing to exercise. Lonely people take more sick days. They're at greater risk for a host of conditions, including heart disease, diabetes, and even dementia.

Loneliness is also mentally damaging. It's exhausting, partly because people who are lonely tend to sleep more lightly and wake up more often during the night. The animal part of our brain is telling us that there aren't any other friendly apes around to warn us when a predator approaches. When we're on our own, we can never fully relax.

Paradoxically, the lonelier we are, the harder it is for us to reach and connect. According to Dr. Stephanie Cacioppo (John Cacioppo's widow and fellow loneliness researcher), lonely people detect threats twice as quickly as people who are less isolated.[25] Night and day, we're stuck in this suspicious mode, looking out for threats. Eventually, we start to perceive other people as threats. We withdraw more and more. Like those prisoners in solitary confinement, even when the door swings open, we're afraid to walk through.

Perhaps that's one reason why we tend to experience loneliness as shameful. The lonely person starts to recoil from other people instinctively. And when we feel vulnerable like that, it's hard for us to open up and share the truth of our experience. Loneliness can become a vicious cycle—the more isolated you are, the harder it is to make real connections. And the fewer connections you have, the lonelier you become.

We seem to be able to sense loneliness in others, too. One study of speed-dating found that people who seemed to be interested in everyone were less desirable to potential partners. In other words, people at this speed-dating event could sense desperation, and it was a huge turn-off.[26] Think about it: you've probably experienced this yourself, whether in a dating context or a broader social context. We're turned off by people who seem too needy. We instinctively shy away from the kid who sits by himself at lunch. The cruel truth of loneliness is that it's self-perpetuating.

Breaking the cycle

Especially if you're already feeling lonely, breaking out of that isolation and making a new connection can seem daunting. Scientists tell us it takes 50 hours of interaction to turn someone from an acquaintance into a friend.[27] (Science really has an answer for everything!) That's why moving and starting over in a new place can be so daunting—you can't rush a deep connection. You have to put in the time.

But there's hope. First, you don't have to go from zero to 50 right away when it comes to establishing more social ties. So-called "weak ties," or acquaintance-level relationships, can have a profound impact on our day-to-day mood and our overall feeling of belonging.[28] Think about the last time you had a brief but genuine moment of connection with a barista, a stranger on public transit, or the person next to you in a yoga class. Didn't it brighten your day? On the flip side, if you spent time socially isolating due to coronavirus, think about how much you missed those little moments of human contact. Social distancing didn't just cut us off from our friends—it cut us off from all those weak ties that make us feel like part of a community.

The other encouraging piece of news about loneliness is that if you're lonely, you don't have to sit around waiting for someone to come and connect with you. In fact, receiving help or support from someone else is actually less likely to combat loneliness than the opposite, according to John Cacioppo. That's why seeing a therapist (while better than nothing) doesn't really make you feel less lonely: we don't actually need support ourselves as much as we need to be embedded in a network of mutual support. "Avoiding loneliness is not about 'getting,' not about being a recipient," as Cacioppo explained in an interview. "If you are only receiving aid and protection from others, that doesn't satisfy this deeper sense of belonging."[29]

We are social animals. We are driven to connect—our brains are literally designed to do this. And ultimately, that desire for connection is as altruistic as it is selfish. What we really want is not just to be cared for, but to care for others. Maybe that's why volunteering is so good for both physical and mental health—because it makes us feel connected to a community and puts us back inside that literally life-sustaining network of mutual care.[30]

Loneliness can be devastating. But combating it is as simple as reaching out and offering a smile, a word of thanks, a helping hand. And the rest of this book will teach you how to make the connections we all need—not with gimmicks or shortcuts, but with serious strategies for establishing trust, combating distraction, and opening up real communication.

PART TWO

THE 5 HABITS OF HUMAN CONNECTION

1

LISTEN
WITHOUT
DISTRACTION

We always have the opportunity to support the people we love by reaching out, leaning in, **and just listening**.

N OCTOBER of 2017, Jim and Sandi Treliving walked into the greenroom at *Breakfast Television Vancouver* ahead of their scheduled live interview on the show. In the television world, the greenroom is where guests go to relax and prepare before their appearances. In my experience, it's almost like a confessional, where guests can get comfortable, open up, and share what's really on their minds.

Jim Treliving is the chairman and owner of Boston Pizza International. He's a successful Canadian entrepreneur—and a "Dragon," known for his long-standing role on the hit reality show *Dragons' Den*, where aspiring entrepreneurs get a chance to pitch their big business ideas. His wife, Sandi, is a force for good in the world as a director on the Foundation Board for the Centre for Addiction and Mental Health (CAMH), Canada's largest mental health teaching hospital.

They were appearing on *Breakfast Television Vancouver* because they were co-chairing the "150 Leading Canadians for Mental Health" campaign in honor of Canada's 150th anniversary. They were there to talk about some Canadians who battled and had overcome mental illness.

I wasn't exactly planning to grill them. Which is why I was so surprised when I walked into the greenroom to say hi, and the first thing Sandi said was, "Riaz, I'm really nervous about going out there. What are you going to ask me?"

"Are you serious?" was my first response, as my initial impression of her was cool confidence. But I knew she needed some reassurance. So I added, "Look, my job is to make you look good and help you share your important message. And let's be real, if I fail, Jim's gonna kick my butt."

We shared a brief laugh, and as I asked them a few more questions, they started to open up about their personal motivations for participating in the campaign. I gave them my full attention.

There's a powerful sense of accountability people experience when in front of the camera. If you're uncomfortable, the viewers will see it—and judge that flop sweat in a hot second. If you're relaxed, there's a real opportunity to share an impactful message and connect with a viewer through the lens.

The goal in all of my conversations, on and off camera, has always been to find a way to make people feel safe. That morning, I could tell Jim and Sandi felt just that as they opened up about their personal lives on live television.

In fact, as Jim described his previous career as an RCMP officer, he started to tell a powerful story about how his nephew, who was 17 years old at the time, had asked to borrow his gun to go hunting. Jim remembers it vividly, because his nephew used that gun to take his own life.

"I should have picked up on it, but I didn't," Jim said.

I could barely breathe listening to this story. I wasn't expecting Jim to open up like that on camera. All he had to do was say a few simple words about the importance of mental health. He could have kept it superficial. Stuck to platitudes. But he took a risk, got vulnerable, and shared something that really mattered. I know I'll never forget it.

How many people in our lives are suffering, but don't show clear symptoms? How many people, like Jim, are left feeling guilty that they didn't see what was happening to someone they loved? We don't always know what's going on inside a person's mind or heart. But we always have the opportunity to support the people we love by reaching out, leaning in, and just listening.

The danger of distraction

Unfortunately, most of the time, most people are pretty terrible listeners. This has been true for decades: back in 1957, Ralph Nichols, a professor at the University of Michigan, and Leonard Stevens, a former public radio newscaster, wrote in the *Harvard Business Review* about some research they'd done on the average person's ability to listen and retain information. They found that *immediately* after hearing someone talk, the average person could only remember half of what they heard.[1]

Nichols also studied kids from first grade to high school. Parents might be surprised to hear that the youngest kids were actually the *best* listeners: 90% of first- and second-graders could tell you exactly what their teacher was just talking about, when asked. Less than half of middle schoolers could do the same, and only about 25% of high schoolers could.[2] It seems that we actually get worse at listening as we get older.

Why? What is it about childhood that makes kids better listeners, and what changes as we age? I'm thinking about my son, Nico. He's almost two. When he focuses on something, he gives it his full attention. It's amazing to watch him investigate a new toy. Amazing... yet annoying at the same time, when I can't get his attention! Seeing the way he focuses on the little things makes me realize how often I'm only giving half of my attention to a task.

Of course, Nico doesn't have a job or bills to pay or anywhere to be by a specific time (that he knows of). He doesn't have to be thinking about what we're going to have for dinner, or whether he's going to be interested in that new toy long enough for me to answer that one email that really needs a reply.

But I think there's something deeper going on, too. It's not just the pressures of adult life that make us so bad at listening. Because even when you completely remove all external distractions, we're bad at listening—to ourselves. In fact, in one study, 67% of men and 25% of women chose to give themselves a mild electric shock rather than sit alone with their thoughts for 15 minutes.[3]

That's pretty astounding. A majority of men and a significant number of women found just sitting still and thinking their own thoughts to be either so boring or so distressing that they chose to shock themselves just for something to do. Something to distract themselves. No wonder most of us are so bad at listening: we don't just happen to get distracted; it's not just an accident—it's something we seek out. Being still, being present in the moment, is actually uncomfortable for many of us.

Now, if you're looking at those electric-shock numbers and thinking that women clearly know something men don't, you're not alone. The gender difference is striking. And it's not just that one study: researchers at Carnegie Mellon University also found that women did significantly better than men on a simple listening test, where they were asked to watch a short video and then answer questions about what they'd heard. Women got 66% of the questions right, but men got only 49%.[4] Compared to women, men also were much more likely to describe themselves as average or below-average listeners.

It would probably take a whole other book to dig into *why* this gender difference exists. My hunch is that it has a lot to do with how men and women are socialized. Women tend to be taught to prioritize relationships, and as any marriage counselor will tell you, listening is key to building success-ful relationships. Power dynamics may play a role, too. We still live in a patriarchal society where men's words are taken more seriously than women's—just ask any woman who's had her suggestion ignored in a meeting, only to have it hailed as genius when a male colleague repeats it a few minutes later. Women may learn to listen out of necessity, while men are still more likely to be able to get away with talking more than they listen.

But whatever the cause, this difference is worth keeping in mind as we dive deeper into listening and distraction. What this gender difference tells us is the ability to listen and be present isn't fixed for all humans at all times. In fact, there's some evidence that socially, we've gotten worse at listening over time. In 1980, a study on college students found that they spent about 53% of their time listening to other people, either one on one or in groups. But in 2006, college kids only spent about 24% of their time listening. Any skill you don't practice will get rusty.

Neuroscience has some explanations for why our brains easily fall prey to the siren song of distraction, but the differ-ences between adults and children, women and men, people in the '80s and people in the 2000s, suggest that who we are and where we are has a big influence on our ability to listen. And that means that listening is something that can be learned and unlearned. That means that even the worst listeners can learn to do better.

What distracts us?

If we want to get better at listening, we've got to learn how to fight distraction. So our first step is to know our enemy. In a typical conversation, what gets in the way of listening? Where does your brain go when you get distracted? Let's look at a few types of distractions in turn.

Working on what you're going to say next

This is an all-too-common problem. You're listening with half your brain, or you think you are—but really, while the other person is talking, you're already thinking about what you're going to say next. The problem here is an excessive focus on your own agenda, according to Leslie Shore, the author of the book *Listen to Succeed*.[5] And that self-focus not only prevents you from processing the information the other person is sharing, but it can also keep you from picking up on their emotional tone.

Formulating a reply instead of truly listening can also be a sign that you're not in the right mindset for the conversation you're having. According to the University of Maryland social psychologist Arie Kruglanski, there are two basic motivational mindsets: thinking and doing.[6] When you're focused on what you're going to say, you're in a doing mindset. You're focused on action. This can lead you into that common conversational trap—offering advice when a person really just wants to be heard. If you're truly listening, you should be in a more reflective thinking mindset.

Emotional distraction

A strong emotional reaction to something someone is saying can also distract us. According to the researchers Nichols and Stevens, this problem can work two ways. First, imagine

Listening is something that can be **learned and unlearned**.

what would happen if your accountant said, "I just got a letter from the IRS." Or if your partner said, "We have to talk." Your emotional reaction to those first few words is likely to make it much harder for you to listen to whatever the person has to say next. It's the same issue that makes it so hard to discuss politics with someone you disagree with—as soon as they say something that makes you angry, you stop listening.

Second, Nichols and Stevens also caution that a positive emotional reaction can undermine your ability to listen by making you too comfortable. When you hear something you strongly agree with, for example, you may essentially tune out and just bathe in the warm feeling of being right. If you're really listening, you should be listening to *everything* the other person is saying, not just the first few words.[7]

Hunger for information

The human brain can process 400 words per minute. But even a very fast speaker will only say about 125 words per minute. That means our brains are about four times as fast as they need to be to handle a normal conversation. And with our big brains, we humans are built to seek as much information as possible. Remember, we evolved from monkeys, who primarily forage for food. Our brains are still wired to reward that kind of hunting and seeking behavior. Learning something new or satisfying curiosity lights up the same reward areas in our brains as food, money, or recreational drugs.[8]

No wonder it's so tempting to think about something else during a long meeting—it's literally not occupying your whole brain. And just a quick peek at your phone might turn up some new piece of information! That's almost as good as eating a Skor Blizzard, minus those extra calories.

Digital distraction

Speaking of phones... if Steve Jobs had put the full power of his big brain to work to purposefully design a device to destroy our ability to listen to one another, he might have come up with something not unlike the iPhone. If our brains were Superman, smartphones would be kryptonite.

Researchers at Carnegie Mellon University wanted to determine just how distracting smartphones really are. So they had three groups of people take a short reading comprehension test. The control group took the test with no interruptions. The other two groups were told that they might get more instructions about the test in a text message. One was actually interrupted with a text, and the other wasn't. But *both* groups did 20% worse on the test than the control group.[9] In other words, simply having a phone out on the table diminished cognitive abilities by 20%.

How often do you have a meal or a drink with a friend with your phone out on the table? Maybe you put it facedown. You think that's going to mean you're not tempted to look at it all the time. It's just there in case you get an urgent message. It's not going to keep you from listening to your friend. Well, this research proves that it will—just by existing, your phone distracts you. Putting your phone on the table during a conversation pretty much guarantees that you won't be able to fully listen to anything that's being said.

Smartphone distraction isn't just something that annoys your friends. It's a massive social problem. The average American looks at their phone 96 times a day. That's once every 10 minutes. The time we waste on our phones at work is estimated to cost companies $15 billion a week. In 2015, more than 391,000 people were injured in distracted-driving accidents. An increasing number of people are actually injured through distracted *walking*.[10]

Remember, just the presence of a phone is distracting enough to reduce your cognitive ability by 20%. But that Carnegie Mellon study also offers some hope. After the first test, the researchers repeated the test. Both groups improved their results the second time around, the interrupted group by 14%, and the warned-but-not-interrupted group by 43%. That means that the second time around, the group that expected to be interrupted but wasn't actually did better than the control group. Knowing they were likely to be interrupted, that "High Alert" group seems to have compensated by working extra hard to concentrate. And it worked!

That finding suggests that it is possible to learn how to be a better listener—even without completely breaking up with our beloved smartphones. Let's explore some strategies for doing just that.

Start by slowing down

Modern life moves at an incredible pace. We're all susceptible to this pressure for speed. When you send an important email, how long does it take for you to start getting impatient for a reply? What about when you send a text message? How soon do you expect a response?

During the coronavirus lockdowns, I posted this question on social media: "What is the best lesson you've learned from the pandemic?" Responses flooded in. Almost every single comment was some kind of variation on "We're actually enjoying each experience we have."

As devastating as it was, for those of us who were able to socially isolate ourselves, the crisis forced us to slow down. We could no longer pack our weeks full of happy hours, dinners, and after-school activities for the kids. We had to subtract so much from our lives. But for many people, those subtractions started to add up to something beautiful: time. Time to watch a movie with our kids. Time to go for a long walk. And yes, time to learn how to bake sourdough bread.

Why did it take a pandemic to make us slow down? What would happen if we kept some of that slow, pared-down spirit, even as the world moves back toward business as usual? By wrenching us out of our routines, the coronavirus pushed many of us to refocus on our true priorities. How can we maintain that focus even as life speeds up again?

Jewish and Christian faith traditions offer one answer: keeping a sabbath. For 24 hours out of the week, believers are asked to stop participating in the busy world of work and commerce. No buying or selling; no work, paid or domestic— nothing but rest, recreation, time with family. This practice feels old-fashioned (and it is, of course, centuries old), but many people have found ways to make it feel relevant, even urgent, in our modern age.

For some people, that means taking a digital sabbath: one day a week to completely avoid all screens. No phone, no laptop, no TV, no video games. Twenty-four hours IRL. Could you do it? What about a 30-day social media fast? Steve Corona, the former CTO of Twitpic, tried it. It took him several days to stop automatically typing "facebook.com" into a new browser tab. But by the end of his experiment, he'd freed up so much time that he started writing a book.[11]

The point is not to demonize our gadgets or make you quit Facebook forever. The point *may* be to radicalize you about the way work has started eating up more and more of our time, to the point where 59% of us check our work email every day *while we're on vacation*, and 50% of us check work email from bed.[12]

But the larger point is to make you be more intentional with how you spend your time and attention. Do you *want* to have half an eye on your inbox while playing with your kids?

If you always know
what you're going
to say next, **you hardly
need to listen at all**.

_____

Is it *possible* to put work aside when you walk through the door and really be present with your family? Could you—don't panic when I say this—*leave your phone at home* when you go to lunch/coffee/happy hour with a friend?

If you do, you'll listen better.

Let go of your agenda

Slowing down and putting away your devices is all well and good when you're trying to focus on coffee with a friend. But what about a really high-stakes conversation? What about a job interview? What about a networking event where you've got maybe three minutes to connect with a bigwig who could be really useful to your career?

When you're coming into a conversation with a clear agenda, it's even more important to really listen to what the other person is saying. The only way you're going to meet your goal in any high-stakes conversation is by making a genuine connection with the other person. Think about it: who would you rather hire, or help—the person who talked at you about their amazing ideas for 15 minutes, or the person who made you feel fascinating by listening carefully to what you had to say?

When I first started out in television, I would go into my interviews armed with a whole list of questions. After all, I'd done my research. I knew what my goals were for the interview. I knew what I wanted them to talk about. It made sense to plan ahead.

But marching through a list of questions cuts off any possibility of genuine connection. If you always know what you're going to say next, you hardly need to listen at all. Eventually I learned that I got much better results by letting go of that list, forgetting my agenda, and opening myself up to actually hear what the person in front of me had to say.

I still do my research before an important conversation. But now I think of it as *over-preparing to improvise*. If I'm doing an interview or meeting an important new contact, I want to know as much as I can about that person. I want to know about their interests, their hobbies, their unique experiences, what they've been tweeting about lately. But the discipline of listening involves putting that aside when they start to talk, so I can open up a space for them to share something I *don't* already know.

By all means, over-prepare for that job interview. Research the company inside and out. Know what the top executives have been tweeting about lately, how last quarter's earnings call went, what the press has been saying about that new product—gather as much information as you can. Prepare some questions and talking points so your mind doesn't go totally blank in the moment. But once the interview begins, let go of that agenda and let yourself be fully present in the conversation. Making a real connection with an interviewer, coming across as an engaged and curious person they might like to work with, is ultimately a far more valuable use of those few minutes than proving that you've rehearsed some good answers to common interview questions.

Over-preparing before an important conversation gives you confidence. Stepping into uncertainty by listening and improvising gives you connection.

Let them lead

Let's get really practical for a second. When I was a morning television host, my favorite way to start a greenroom conversation with a guest was to simply ask, "What's on your mind?"

I like this question because it's open-ended, and it allows the other person to tell me where they want the conversation to go. It's respectful; rather than opening with my agenda, I'm leaving space for them to tell me what they'd like to talk about. Feel like a familiar exercise? Facebook asks you this same question as soon as you open up your profile.

People will surprise you. When Geroy Simon, a former star football player for the BC Lions, came on the show in 2017, it was a different conversation than expected. He was Mr. Charisma when he was on the team, and then he went on to serve as the team's director of Canadian scouting. He was basically an ambassador for the team. He was appearing on the show to talk about the upcoming season. Standard stuff.

But I also knew that his wife had died three months before. And when I walked into the greenroom, I could see by his body language that putting that aside and just doing a standard, upbeat interview about the team was going to be a heavy lift for him. So I said to him: "People care about you, man. And I want you to feel safe out there. What would you like to share about your wife, if people are wondering how you're doing?"

He told me how brutal this life transition had been. He hadn't shared a lot about his struggle publicly. But it was obviously weighing on his heart. And in that moment, just by asking him what he wanted to share, it gave him an opportunity to open up and be real.

On camera, Geroy decided just to share how much he appreciated all the fans showing their support for him and his family. But I'll never forget that human moment we had in the greenroom.

Your question can be simple. "What's on your mind?" "What are you struggling with?" "What would you like to share?" Just by asking, and waiting with an open mind for an answer, you're creating a space for that person to be as real as they need to be.

Before my father died, when I knew someone had suffered a loss, I used to be terrified of saying the wrong thing. I think that's why we so often fall back on stock phrases like "I'm sorry for your loss," or "Let me know if there's anything I can do to help." We're afraid that if we say the wrong thing, we'll somehow make it worse—but what could make grief worse? Maybe what we're really afraid of is the raw grief itself. We're afraid of getting too close to it. We're afraid that the wrong word will make the person in front of us completely fall apart, and we don't think we can handle that kind of vulnerability.

Now that I've gone through that kind of powerful grief myself, I know that I've failed all those people who could have used some comfort. By holding back, afraid of saying the wrong thing, I've failed to make a genuine connection at the moment those people needed it most.

One of the most valuable conversations I've ever had happened four months after losing my father. I was hosting the annual "Gift of Love" fundraising gala, which supports Canuck Place Children's Hospice in British Columbia. Being a parent, the cause is one that's close to my heart. The devastating stories parents have the courage to share about how they lost their children are simply heartbreaking. Sitting at the table beside Deborah, one of the lead family counselors from Canuck Place, I listened as she described how she does her job and connects with families coping with grief and loss.

LISTEN WITHOUT DISTRACTION

I asked her, "Deborah, what's the best thing you can say to someone who is grieving?"

She opened my eyes with her response. "It's not about what you can say, it's about what you can ask. Allow them to share something meaningful. The one thing I do to create a safe space for them to share is to ask them one very important thing: 'What do you want me to know about them?'" What a beautiful question.

During the coronavirus crisis, I saw CNN's Chris Cuomo interview someone who had just lost her brother to the virus. He asked her, "What do you want people to know about this beautiful human being?" The response was a gripping conversation on life and family, along with powerful and personal storytelling.

Now, when I encounter someone who's grieving, that's what I ask: "What do you want me to know about them?" This question leaves space for the grieving person to talk about their loss in whatever way they want to at that moment. It shows you're willing to hear what's on their mind. And you could ask the same basic question during other hard times in a person's life—a job loss, a breakup. "What do you want me to know about what you're going through right now?" It's simple, it's respectful, and it leaves space for them to lead the conversation wherever they need it to go.

Five ways to listen more deeply

OK, so you've slowed yourself down. You've put your agenda aside, and you're willing to let the other person lead the conversation. How do you actually listen in that deep way that creates a real connection?

It sounds like a simple question. Well, you just... listen. You put your phone down, you stop thinking about other things, and you listen. But if being a good listener were easy, we'd all be doing it already.

Over the course of my career, I've developed five strategies that help me listen more carefully and uncover a deeper level in any conversation. Let's walk through them each in turn.

Let go of your assumptions

If you think you know what someone is going to say, you're not really listening. On the one hand, if I'd gone into that conversation with Geroy Simon assuming that he only wanted to talk about the team and the upcoming season, I would have missed out on an opportunity to make a real connection in the midst of a busy workday. On the other hand, I've interviewed plenty of people who've suffered and struggled, and they don't always want to dig in and get deep and display their suffering for the world to see. Sometimes they want to keep it relatively light and stick to their talking points. Only by letting go of our assumptions about what we think the conversation is going to be like can we actually be present in and listen to the conversation we're actually having.

Listen for repetition

I recently had dinner with a potential new business connection. This was supposed to be a casual, get-to-know-you, maybe-we-can-work-together kind of chat. But I noticed as we were talking that he used the word "ex" three times within the first few minutes. That suggested to me that this was something that was weighing on his mind. So the next time he mentioned his ex, I asked a follow-up question. Turned out he had just gotten divorced. So we talked about that—and made a much deeper connection than we otherwise would have.

You can do this in any conversation: listen for words or phrases that the person is repeating. These might be clues

Ask, "What do you want me to know about what you're **going through right now**?"

about what's really going on with them. If you ask a respectful, open-ended question about that topic, you'll leave space for them to open up if they want to.

Embrace their emotional intensity

Another clue that can lead you to a deeper level of connection is emotional intensity. Whether the person you're talking to is getting excited or angry, beaming or tearing up, heightened emotion is a sign that you're touching on a topic that really matters to them.

Many cultures teach us to shy away from strong emotion. If you ever watched the HBO show *Six Feet Under*, you may remember the conversation the two brothers have in the pilot about the little side room in the funeral parlor. Any time a mourner starts to break down, they're whisked away behind a curtain, so they don't upset everyone else. As if people at a funeral aren't, by definition, already upset. We do that so often with strong emotions—we draw a curtain over them. We tell the people around us it's not that big a deal, or it could be worse.

Alternatively, sometimes strong emotion in others provokes strong emotion in us. When we're talking politics at Thanksgiving, and Uncle Phil starts to raise his voice, we raise our voice in response. It's instinctual—but it doesn't help. Nobody wins the argument. Nobody's convinced on either side.

The next time you see someone expressing strong emotion, try not to shy away from it *or* let it provoke you. Instead, get curious about it. Say something like "I can see this means a lot to you." Ask a question like "Why is this issue so important for you?" or "Is there more?" And really listen to the response instead of trying to fix it.

Listen with your eyes

When I'm interviewing someone, or having a pre-interview chat in the greenroom, I'm looking at every single aspect of what they're giving me from the moment we start talking. I'm listening for tone, I'm taking their emotional temperature, and I'm watching their body language for clues.

Body language can tell us so much about how another person is feeling. And you don't have to be a highly trained FBI interrogator to unpack what a person's posture and gestures are saying. Reading body language is instinctual for most of us. We just have to pay attention to what our instincts are telling us.

Try it the next time you're having a casual conversation with a friend or coworker. Take a moment to notice the way that they're holding their body. Look for obvious clues, like a person tilting their head to indicate interest or crossing their arms to protect themselves. But also take note of how *you're* feeling in that moment. Do you feel warm and connected? Defensive and shut off? Chances are, you're instinctively responding to something in their tone or body language. And the more you stop to notice body language, the better you'll get at deliberately reading it.

Maintain a beginner's mind

"In the beginner's mind there are many possibilities, but in the expert's there are few."

That's the first line of the book *Zen Mind, Beginner's Mind* by the teacher Shunryu Suzuki.[13] These few words capture so much wisdom. When we feel we know a lot about a subject, we can become closed off to possibilities. We feel like we know what will work and what won't, what's possible and what isn't. Beginner's mind is powerful because it keeps you open to learning something in every conversation.

I once interviewed Ron MacLean, the well-known host from *Hockey Night in Canada*. He told me that there are always two teachers in any conversation: the person who's speaking is teaching something, but the listener can teach, too, with the way they listen and accept.

I took those words to heart. As an interviewer, I always tried to approach my interviews with a beginner's mind. I do tons of research before every interview, but when I begin a conversation, I put that information out of my mind and come in with authentic curiosity.

You don't have to be a professional interviewer or a Zen master to go into a conversation with a beginner's mind. Try this: before a conversation, think to yourself, "I wonder what this person has to teach me." Or, "I wonder what this person wants to talk about." Cultivate that spirit of curiosity and see where it takes you. (We'll dig deeper into curiosity in the next chapter.)

Beginner's mind is helpful in any conversation but can be particularly powerful in conversation with someone you know well. When you assume you know everything about a person, you operate on autopilot and shut off the possibility of discovering another part of them. You close off any opportunity for them to surprise you. What if you went into your next conversation with your partner, your best friend, your parent, or your child with a beginner's mind?

Ask, don't tell

Listening takes practice. Distractions are everywhere in our lives, and they aren't going away. Be patient with yourself. If you're in a conversation and you notice your mind is wandering, just take a breath and refocus.

When in doubt, always come back to "how" and "what" questions. Instead of trying to fix someone's problem, ask another question. Instead of giving advice, ask a question. Instead of interrupting to promote yourself, ask a question. If you feel the need to challenge the other person's ideas, listen first. Ask clarifying questions to make sure you understand their position. Then share your counterpoint.

An active listener asks the questions that help someone discover the meaning behind their own personal experiences. Let's look at some real-world examples:

- If you're giving feedback, start by asking "How do you feel that went?" Let them validate themselves, then dig deeper with follow-up questions.

- If you're stuck in conflict, ask "What do you think *won't* happen? How could you make it happen?"

- If you want to encourage empathy, ask "How could I show up for you more?"

- If you want to encourage them to draw a lesson from their experience, ask "What would you do differently if you had to do it over again?"

- If you feel like you're not connecting, call yourself out by asking "What question have I failed to ask to understand your perspective?"

When in doubt, come back to questions. Research shows that listening is about more than just quietly accepting what someone else is saying; we perceive those who ask thoughtful questions to be good listeners.[14] Part of listening is participating in the conversation—asking questions, reflecting, and pushing the other person to clarify their thinking. A good listener isn't just passive. Their curiosity is fully present in the conversation.

2

MAKE YOUR SMALL TALK BIGGER

When you lead with authentic curiosity, you **create room for unexpected connections**.

ONE NIGHT in August 2016, Lori came home and found me listening to Ozzy Osbourne. Kind of a surprise, since she knows I'm a '90s hip-hop and R&B guy. Usher and Ginuwine are usually in regular rotation on my playlists.

So she started laughing. "What are you doing?" she asked me.

"Research," I said. "Zakk Wylde is on the show tomorrow."

Her jaw dropped. I could see real concern in her eyes. She did not think I was ready for this. Honestly, I didn't think so either. "Tell him your wife is a big fan," she said after a moment. "And tell him I listen to Morbid Angel."

I had no idea what those words meant. And I could hear her laughing at me as she walked away. Didn't exactly make me more confident about the interview.

For the record, Zakk Wylde is a revered guitarist who played with Ozzy Osbourne and is also the lead singer of the heavy metal band Black Label Society.

The next morning, Zakk showed up dressed in full leather and smelling of man musk. Was I nervous? Yes. Curious? Absolutely. Slightly terrified of making a fool of myself on live television? Without a doubt. Turns out Zakk was one of the nicest, kindest guests I've ever interviewed. From the moment we met in the greenroom, I owned up to the fact that I'm not exactly a metalhead. Not that my pocket square wasn't a dead giveaway that we were from different worlds...

I told him Lori said hi, and that she told me to listen to Morbid Angel before the interview. He thought that was hilarious.

I still don't know what that means.

This was a big interview for the show. Zakk was a big name. I had manically over-prepared with research because I felt so unprepared on a basic level—here I was, getting ready to talk to a music legend, but I was totally lacking the gut-level sense of *why* this guy was so important to so many people. I could read about his legendary career, I could listen to his music, but nothing could turn me into a metalhead overnight.

So I did my homework. When the cameras started rolling, I was nervous. I have to admit, I was too focused on my research and my own nerves to really relax and go with the flow of the conversation. I was obsessing about making sure I asked all my questions and gave him the chance to talk about all the great stuff he's creating.

I think Zakk knew I was nervous. I'm pretty sure that's why he threw out the words "anal bleaching" within the first 40 seconds of the interview.

Yes, you read that right. That's the rock star lifestyle, I guess.

Thanks to Zakk's colorful comments, that was one of the highest-rated online *Breakfast Television Vancouver* segments in 2016. But it was after the interview that we really connected. We ended up shooting a video on my phone for Lori, and when I confessed that I'd never actually been to a heavy metal show, he invited me to his show that night. Lori told me not to wear a pocket square.

It was amazing watching Zakk perform from backstage. The energy at the Commodore Ballroom in Vancouver was electric as thousands of people worshipped him for the rock god he truly is. He actually played his guitar with his teeth!

I'm still a hip-hop and R&B guy at heart, but I loved getting a glimpse of Zakk in his element. Who knew two people from such different worlds could hit it off so well? When you lead with authentic curiosity, you create room for unexpected connections.

First impressions

For someone like me, who values the intimacy of a one-on-one conversation over a cocktail party, it's not always easy meeting new people. And I'm pretty sure I'm not alone. Researchers from Columbia University studied what actually happened at a networking event. They found that people mostly spent time with friends they already knew—even though they had gone into the event for the purpose of meeting new people.

It may be the networking itself. Another study found that when people engaged in "instrumental networking" and tried to connect with people with a goal of advancing their career, they literally felt dirty, to the point that they wanted to take a shower. But networking is essential. As many as 85% of jobs are filled through networking, and 70% to 80% of jobs are never even advertised—they're filled by internal candidates or through personal networks.[1]

And, of course, meeting new people isn't just about finding a job. You have to meet new people in order to date, make friends, and build community. Meeting new people introduces you to new ideas. Making a new connection could steer you toward a new hobby or a new passion—or expose you to a point of view you hadn't considered before.

When we do meet new people, we form an impression of them incredibly quickly. One study found that people were able to gather a fairly reliable impression of a stranger's

trustworthiness after seeing their face for just 33 millisec-
onds. "Reliable" in this case means similar to the judgments
formed by people who were allowed to look at the faces as
long as they wanted. So what the study shows is not necessarily that our instincts about people are completely accurate in
some impartial, universal sense, but simply that we do form
our first impressions of people very quickly—in a literal split
second. And we make that split-second judgment, in large
part, by reading nonverbal signals: things like posture, cloth-
ing, and handshakes all have a big impact on that first read
of a new person.[2]

But if our judgment of new people were based *only* on that
first split-second impression, Zakk Wylde would never have
invited me backstage at his show. Pocket square, meet leather
cuffs—not exactly the beginning of a beautiful friendship.

Zakk and I came from completely different worlds. We
had nothing in common. How did we form a connection?
How did we get past the barrier thrown up by that split-
second first impression, and figure out that we could actually
enjoy each other's company?

Authentic curiosity is the key

In the last chapter, we discussed the importance of asking
good questions. In this chapter, we're going to dig deeper
into curiosity—what it is, what makes it so powerful, and
how you can use it to get past the small talk stage and build a
real connection when you meet someone new.

Scientists have identified at least two types of curiosity:
diversive curiosity, which is the generalized thirst for knowledge that drives us to hunt for new information or dive down
a Wikipedia rabbit hole; and epistemic curiosity, which is

the more sustained and purposeful drive to fully understand a subject.[3] Diversive curiosity makes us gobble up "fun facts" like a chipmunk filling his cheeks with nuts, while epistemic curiosity is what makes scientists, explorers, and artists tick. Mario Livio, the author of the book *Why? What Makes Us Curious*, identifies a third type: perceptual curiosity.[4] This is the curiosity we feel when we learn something that doesn't seem to fit with what we thought we knew. A surprise like that throws us off and drives us to hunt for more information to make the world make sense again.

Livio's research suggests that curiosity can be unpleasant at times—the "hang on, that can't be right" feeling. Curiosity can also fuel dangerous behavior. That basic desire for novelty can be part of what drives thrill-seeking. It's also part of what makes us watch gory movies, listen to true crime podcasts, or turn to look at an accident on the side of the road. We know it's going to be bad, but *how* bad? Bad in what way? We have to know.

In one study, researchers left participants in a room with a bunch of pens, some of which they were told could deliver a small electric shock. For one group, the pens were color-coded—red pens were "live" and green pens were safe. For the other group, all pens were yellow. The yellow-pen group tested more pens, indicating that the uncertainty kept them more interested longer.[5]

In our personal lives, this drive to *know* even at a cost can cause us real pain. It's what pushes us to look up an ex on Instagram and see how happy they are with their new partner. Think of Pandora's box—sometimes, even knowing it will cause real harm, we just have to know. We can't look away.

But for the most part, curiosity is a positive drive. Curious people tend to be happier. They tend to enjoy school and work more, and do better in both. In general, older people tend to be less curious than younger folks. But those older people who retain their curiosity tend to do better on memory tests and other mental tests.[6] Curiosity seems to help stave off some of the mental decline of old age.

In business, curiosity has many benefits. Because curiosity prompts us to look for more options, curious people tend to make better decisions. Curiosity also leads to more creativity and innovation. And that's not just useful for artists or entrepreneurs—one study of call-center workers found that the more curious employees were more likely to ask their coworkers questions, which made them better at their jobs and helped them come up with more creative solutions to customer problems.[7]

Curious teams also work better together. Curious people communicate better and get involved in less conflict. They tend to be less aggressive. They enjoy socializing more, and they're more resilient when faced with rejection.[8]

In the end, authentic curiosity builds better relationships. One study by researcher Todd Kashdan found that curious people both expected more out of conversations with people they didn't know, and felt closer to those new people after a brief conversation. Another Kashdan study looked at the other side of the equation, and found that people rated curious conversation partners as more attractive, and felt closer to them.[9]

Barriers to curiosity

The itch to know more is innate and can be incredibly beneficial. But in a world where Wikipedia exists, we never have to spend much time in that state of not-knowing. You've probably experienced this yourself: if you're old enough to remember a world before smartphones, you know that, in those days, a group of friends at a dinner party or pub night could easily spend 15 minutes debating what voice actor has been in every Pixar movie. Today, the answer is just a Google search away. For all you trivia buffs, I'll save you a step. It's John Ratzenberger.[10]

The convenience of having all the world's information at our fingertips at all times is a powerful lure. It's part of the larger culture of convenience technology has created. We can order almost anything we can think of from Amazon and have it in our hands within 24 hours. We can get food from almost any restaurant to our door within an hour.

And technology doesn't just fetch us things—in many cases, it actually does the thinking for us. Netflix tells us what other people who watch the shows we watch have been watching, so we don't have to decide what to watch next. Delivery apps show us the most popular dishes so we don't have to sort through a restaurant's menu ourselves. Google Maps removes the need to remember how to get anywhere. Google search has gotten so sophisticated that we no longer have to type out a whole question: just a few keywords will get you the answer you need. And once you get that answer, your curiosity disappears. You no longer need to think about that topic. According to Amit Singhal, Google's former head of search, "The more accurate the machine gets, the lazier the questions become."[11]

Removing the need for actual thought—is that the ultimate convenience? Tim Wu, the author of *The Attention Merchants: The Epic Scramble to Get inside Our Heads*, has written that convenience "has emerged as perhaps the most powerful force shaping our individual lives and our economies" today. And Evan Williams, the cofounder of Twitter, has gone even further: "Convenience decides everything."[12]

But technology isn't the only thing standing between us and all the benefits of curiosity. Even though the vast majority of businesspeople recognize the importance of curiosity, few workplaces are actually set up to encourage curiosity in practical ways. Many leaders worry that letting people explore, daydream, and innovate will somehow slow down decision-making. And the constant pressure to be productive, to grind out the work on your to-do list, undermines your ability to think big and your drive to ask the questions that lead to original thought.

In the modern, Western world, too much information may be killing our curiosity, but in other times and places, powerful people have restricted access to information to try to keep people from asking "why." In the Middle Ages, for example, the church worked to make knowledge and exploration the privilege of a few. Mario Livio, the author of *Why?*, has also argued that repressive regimes like the Nazis and the Taliban have destroyed art and books as a way to stamp out that human drive to explore and learn.[13]

How to encourage curiosity: for yourself

Curiosity is a natural human drive. But circumstances and habits can either encourage or stifle it. The good news is, that means that you can train yourself to be more curious.

Start with a simple, but powerful, 10-second exercise, designed by neuroscientist Jud Brewer:[14] If you find yourself feeling frustrated or anxious (two strong emotions that are likely to close off curiosity), take note of how wide-open your eyes are. Now deliberately open your eyes very wide. See what happens to that negative emotion. According to Brewer, we instinctively open our eyes wide when we're curious and

In a world where
Wikipedia exists,
we never have to spend
much time **in that
state of not-knowing**.

narrow them when we're angry, so opening your eyes wide can help jump-start your curiosity.

Here are some other tips for cultivating curiosity:

Deliberately seek out new or surprising experiences. It's harder to cultivate curiosity when you're stuck in a well-worn routine.[15] Try a new restaurant; take a class in something you know nothing about; ask a friend to introduce you to a hobby you've never tried.

Admit when you don't know something. Putting up a false front is only going to prevent you from learning something new.

Research an unfamiliar topic. How long has it been since you picked up a book and read about something totally new to you? Indulge your inner nine-year-old and read up on dinosaurs, pyramids, space travel, or whatever strikes your fancy. Check out the work of science writer Mary Roach—I will literally bet you $5 that at least one of her books will spark your curiosity.

Make learning a game. Games encourage curiosity.[16] Play an online trivia game, challenge yourself to advance a level in Duolingo, or create your own game and award yourself points for every new fun fact you learn.

Set aside time for curiosity practice. You could try people-watching with a notebook in hand to write down your observations. You could brainstorm solutions to everyday problems. You could challenge yourself to come up with "what if" questions about a product you use every day: what if this were bigger/smaller/disposable/recyclable/rentable? The more you practice entering the mental space of curiosity, the more natural it will feel.[17]

How to encourage curiosity: with your partner

When you get comfortable, curiosity can fade, and you can slip into autopilot mode. To continue thriving in your relationship, keep seeking surprises and resist the urge to surrender to mundane check-in questions like "How was your day?" or "What do you want for dinner?"

Many studies have provided some powerful cues to build a deeper connection with a partner. In one famous study by the psychologist Arthur Aron, strangers asked one another 36 questions designed to guide them toward greater intimacy by encouraging vulnerability. You can use these questions with a partner to deepen your connection.[18] Here's a sampling:

- For what in your life do you feel most grateful?
- If you could change anything about the way you were raised, what would it be?
- If you could wake up tomorrow having gained any one quality or ability, what would it be?
- Is there something that you've dreamed of doing for a long time? Why haven't you done it?
- If you knew that in one year you would die suddenly, would you change anything about the way you are now living? Why?
- Make three true "we" statements each. For instance, "We are both in this room feeling..."
- Tell your partner what you like about them; be very honest this time, saying things that you might not say to someone you've just met.
- Share with your partner an embarrassing moment in your life.

- If you were to die this evening with no opportunity to communicate with anyone, what would you most regret not having told someone? Why haven't you told them yet?

How to encourage curiosity: on a team

Curiosity is also contagious, so encouraging curiosity in the people around you will reinforce your own efforts to cultivate curiosity. If you're in a leadership role at work (or in an organization you volunteer with), there's a lot you can do to foster curiosity on your team. Here are some strategies leaders can use to promote creativity at work:[19]

Be curious when interviewing. Eric Schmidt, Google's former CEO, once said, "We run this company on questions, not answers." The company's famously oddball interview questions (like "Have you ever found yourself unable to stop learning about something?") were purposely designed to identify people who approach problems with a spirit of curiosity and even playfulness. You don't have to test people with brain-teasers, though—just look for people who ask good questions and seem to genuinely want to know more about how your office works.

If you are the one being interviewed for a job or big contract, one powerful question you can ask at the end of the conversation is "Given what we've discussed, what might prevent you from hiring me for this opportunity?" It's bold, yet the response will allow you to understand and speak to any hesitations.

Be a curiosity role model. If people see their leaders taking the time to ask questions, explore alternative options, and brainstorm off-the-wall solutions, they'll learn that curiosity is a valued asset on the team.

Encourage ongoing learning. Many companies have discovered the value of providing education benefits to employees. These programs increase employee engagement and decrease turnover, and they also signal to your teams that the organization values learning.

Let people "slack off" occasionally. We're back to Google again—their program allowing employees to spend 20% of their time exploring personal projects actually ended up creating some of the company's most innovative products.[20]

Brainstorm for questions, not answers. For a really great brainstorming session, invite some people from outside your team, challenge everyone in the room to come up with as many *questions* on a topic as possible within a set amount of time, and make a strict rule that there are *no answers allowed* during this time.[21]

How to encourage curiosity: for your kids

Modern parenting has become a high-pressure activity. Many parents are understandably worried that today's world is so competitive that their kids can't afford to fail—so they push kids toward academic achievement at a very young age. But a high-stress environment is actually a great way to kill curiosity. Here are some ways parents (and teachers) can encourage kids to be curious:[22]

Give them unstructured time. If you do nothing else, do this one thing. Unstructured, child-directed play is actually the best way for young kids to learn about the world. Put aside the enriching activities and let your kid make a mess. Don't direct them—sit back and let them take the lead.

When you first
meet someone, make
your mantra
**" 'Look at you' needs
to be greater than
'look at me.' "**

———

Encourage reading for pleasure. Reading is a great way to explore new ideas and learn about a wide range of topics. Check out the book *How to Raise a Reader* by Maria Russo and Pamela Paul for a host of age-appropriate suggestions. But know that the best way to encourage your kids to read is to model it yourself. Keep plenty of books in the house (libraries have them for free!) and let your kids see you reading for fun.

Answer their questions. When your kid asks a question, even if you're trying to get dinner on the table, force yourself to slow down and stay in the moment with them. Answer the question as best you can. If you don't know the answer, research it together. Model investigation and reward curiosity with engagement.

Ask them some questions. Nudge them to wonder and speculate about the world around them. Ask "what if" together. Try to be a curiosity role model—ask them some questions you don't know the answer to.

Curiosity in conversation

OK, so you've spent some time cultivating curiosity in yourself and the people around you. You're now a wide-eyed, wonderstruck, question-asking machine. How do you take that beautiful spirit of curiosity and bring it back down to earth? How does curiosity actually become useful in the context of a conversation? How does curiosity help you build connections, particularly with people you don't know?

When you first meet someone, make your mantra "'Look at you' needs to be greater than 'look at me.'" Yes, this was the great advice I got at the beginning of my career. This will help you build trust, as people are unconsciously asking themselves three key questions about you in your initial encounter:

- Do you care about me?
- Are you listening to me?
- Can I trust you?

Remember, humans are social animals. When we encounter someone new, we're instinctively trying to decide whether they're a friend or a foe. That's true when you're meeting someone socially—whether you're aware of it or not, you're sizing them up and trying to decide whether or not you want to spend more time with them.

Those unconscious questions are particularly important in a professional context. At a networking event, for example, many people literally are evaluating everyone they meet. And if you work in sales or customer service, you probably already know that customers tend to approach you warily, wondering if you're really listening to them, or just trying to run through a script as quickly as possible and get to the sale or get them off the phone.

A spirit of curiosity is crucial to getting a "yes" to these unconscious questions. Curious people care about the world around them. They listen intently because they know that everyone has an interesting story to share. And they come across as trustworthy precisely because of that careful, open-minded listening. In the context of a conversation, curiosity is a choice—it's an intention to learn more. Genuine curiosity requires you to let go of judgment and open yourself to understanding the world as it is. And you demonstrate that curiosity by asking great questions.

How to ask great questions

Great questions get great answers. When it comes to asking a great question, my experience interviewing countless experts has taught me that there is no one-size-fits-all formula. Context is key. You've got to be brief, ask open-ended questions, and above all put the focus on the other person, or the idea being shared. Here are my best tips for asking excellent questions:

Get to the point

Be concise and direct, and get to the point as quickly as possible. One of the common traps we fall into is starting with a long-drawn-out introduction or complicated setup consisting of multiple questions. That's a great way to overwhelm the person you're talking to and leave them unable to answer *any* of your questions. Keeping things simple will actually leave more room to take the conversation deeper.

Dig deep with follow-up questions

The first answer you get is almost always the appetizer for the main course. To truly connect with others, develop an insatiable appetite for follow-up questions.

This isn't something you can always prepare for. Depending on the situation, when you meet someone new, you may be able to prepare two or three thoughtful questions in advance. But good follow-up has to be done on the fly. It requires giving someone your undivided attention and picking up on the cues they're giving you.

When you hear something interesting—and if you're listening in a spirit of curiosity, lots of things you hear should be interesting—try asking, "Could you elaborate on that?" or "Could you tell me more about the stance you're taking?"

If you're not sure you understand their point, or you want to make sure you aren't misinterpreting them, recap what you think their point of view is, and then ask, "Is that what you're saying?" Or go back to basics and simply ask "Why?" and then ask "Why?" again.

Forget about your next planned question and have the courage to step into uncertainty with your curiosity. This will show that you listened, that you care, and that you want to learn more.

Ask for specific stories, not just answers

This all comes down to emotion. Peter Guber's book *Tell to Win* outlines the power of emotion. It is what connects us, it is what polarizes us, and it is what motivates us to act. The best way to connect to emotion is to tell someone a story—or ask them to tell you one. Our brains absorb stories as if we are experiencing them ourselves, so stories are a powerful way to build deeper connections.

My first big interview, back when I started my career on MTV Canada, was Shaggy. Yes, Mr. Lover Lover. A big-name interview like that comes with a lot of pressure. Fans want to get a glimpse of the real person behind the music they love. I was anxious going in, but Shaggy put me at ease. Seventeen years later, I got the chance to interview him again. I'd learned a lot by then about how to ask better questions and leave more space for my interview subject to shine. This time, knowing that he had toured in Europe with James Brown, I simply asked him: "Tell us the story about the advice James Brown gave you about your talent."

Shaggy said that James Brown watched every single one of his performances. It made him a little nervous, because James Brown was a formidable figure on the tour. Everyone called him Mr. Brown, but Shaggy got away with calling him

Godfather. But one day Mr. Brown came into Shaggy's dressing room and told him—and I wish you could hear Shaggy's James Brown impression, because it was legendary—"I watch you every night. You, you're the truth. Let me tell you one thing: they can take away your woman, your house, your car, but they can never take your talent. So long as you've got your talent, you're a rich man."

Asking for stories can be that simple, and that rewarding. Remember, people love to talk about themselves. Most people don't need much prompting. As long as they can see you're genuinely curious, they'll open up and share.

If you want someone to share a story, ask about their reactions to specific moments and consider these three themes:

1 **Trials:** Think about tapping into the emotion behind the surface-level highlight reel we all tend to share when we're meeting someone for the first time. Ask:
   "When was the last time you did something for the first time?"
   "How did it feel to try something new?"
   "What was the hardest part about [building your business/ learning a language/etc.]?"

2 **Transitions:** Think about the uncertainty the person you're talking to might be facing. Ask:
   "What did it feel like to make that change?"
   "How did you overcome adversity and manage that unpredictable situation?"
   "How did you adapt to your new reality?"

3 **Triumphs:** Let the person you're talking to share a moment of glory. Ask:
   "How did it feel to hit that milestone?"
   "What was your formula for success?"
   "How has your success [winning an award/becoming a mentor/ etc.] changed the way you look at life?"

What is the most important conversation **you've had in your life**?

Suspend your judgment

It's all too easy to subtly express a point of view or indicate the answer you're expecting in a question, without even realizing it. Always strive for open-ended questions that leave room for the person to share something you're not expecting. Think "How did that feel?" rather than "That must have been difficult."

Imagine you were a small business owner trying to survive the coronavirus. You could have been asking stakeholders: "Should we close the business now or should we continue on with layoffs so we can survive this tough stretch?" Or, you could have asked: "What do you think we should do here?" The second question leaves much more room for the other person to jump in with a creative idea or even just share how they're feeling in an uncertain time.

Sometimes we are so eager to demonstrate our understanding that we don't take enough time to really listen to what the other person is saying. Say you're at a professional conference. You're talking to someone you just met, and they comment that it's been a long day packed with information. You want to connect with them, so you jump in and say, "I know, aren't you just exhausted?"

It's not a terrible thing to say. Pleasant chitchat can continue. But what if you had said, "Yeah, I'm pretty wiped out. How are you feeling?" Maybe they would have responded, "Honestly, I'm energized—it's my first work trip since my kid was born." By asking an open-ended question, instead of assuming you know how they feel, you might create an opportunity to take the conversation deeper. As Peter Bregman, the author of *Leading with Emotional Courage*, has written, you have to *develop* your understanding of another person before you can *demonstrate* it.[23]

If you can suspend your judgment and your advice and keep things open, you invite the person in front of you to think creatively and express themselves in a deeper, more genuine way.

Use silence as your secret weapon

You ask a question. There's a pause. You're nervous. Your brain starts churning—"Was that a stupid question? Have I offended them? Oh my God, this is a disaster!" Panicking, you jump in with a clarification, or another question, or a total change of subject. And you cut off the opportunity to get a real answer.

That initial pause after you ask a question may feel awkward, but it could also be a really good sign that the person is taking time to reflect on the idea you just introduced. The easy thing to do is to immediately throw in filler words or questions to curb that all-important silence. But when you do that, you miss a potentially profound response.

Throw out the question, give them your attention, and let silence do the talking. Watch what happens.

My favorite question

After 17 years of asking questions for a living, I've seen a lot. Once you've heard the words "anal bleaching" on live television, there's not much left that can surprise you. I've interviewed people from all walks of life and discussed topics both trivial and profound. I've asked thousands of questions over the course of my career.

Here is my number one favorite question to ask (and yes, you can steal it!):

What is the most important conversation you've had in your life?

I asked Evander Holyfield that question. The Real Deal opened up about his mother reminding him that family is the foundation of everything in life.

I asked hockey legend Bobby Orr that question. He started playing organized hockey when he was just eight years old, and racked up an incredible number of records and trophies until his professional career was cut short by knee problems.[24] He told me the most important conversations he has are when he talks to parents about letting their kids be kids, and not pushing them to professionalize their athletics too soon.

I asked the late Dr. Wayne Dyer that question the week of his 74th birthday. A prolific author and speaker in the fields of motivation, spirituality, and self-improvement, Dyer actually told me that every year on his birthday his most important conversation came from a question he asked himself. "Did I live 74 years, or did I live the same year 74 times?" I will never forget the power of this reflection. He was diagnosed with leukemia in 2012, but died three years later, at the age of 75, from a heart attack.[25] I can only hope that I live my last years—all my years—as thoughtfully and intentionally as he did.

Not every conversation we have is going to be life-changing. But every conversation has the potential to change a life. Relationships are built in conversations. And what matters more, in the end, than relationships?

Too often, we think of small talk as tedious, something we have to get through—to be polite, to start off small, to get our foot in the door with a new person. We talk about the weather or ask rote questions, like the dreaded "What do you do?"

But small talk doesn't have to be small. When you first meet a new person, you have no idea what they might be able to teach you. Why not approach new people with a spirit of authentic curiosity? Why not ask real questions—not to put the other person on the spot, but because you genuinely want to know what they have to say?

You never know what someone might have to teach you. You never know which conversation will be the most important in your life. Stay open. Stay curious. You never know what you're going to hear.

3

PUT ASIDE YOUR PERFECT PERSONA

———

Real connection
isn't about perfection.
Real connection
comes from **the
ability to embrace
imperfection**.

WHEN ONE of the world's most famous illusionists came to Vancouver, his people set up a marathon session of 10 interviews in a row. I was with MTV Canada, and we were lucky number 10.

When I came into the room, I could feel he was tired, but he still gave me a warm welcome. I'd done my research, and I knew this guy had just bought some property in the Bahamas—and he was a hip-hop fan. I wasn't planning on asking him about that stuff, but I had that information in my back pocket in case I needed it.

His latest touring show was all about dreams coming true. A great topic. But when the interview started, he was giving me one-word answers. His energy was flagging after doing nine other interviews on the same topic. I knew I needed to liven things up, or I'd have nothing.

Finally, he flipped the script and asked me what my dream was. And I knew I had to come up with something quick to salvage this.

"Well listen, I'm sipping on piña coladas on the beach in the Bahamas," I said, "and you're there with me, man."

In that moment, I could see a spark in his eye. "You know I just bought property in the Bahamas, right?" he asked. I went along for the ride: "Really? Get the hell out of here. No way... tell me more."

Next thing you know, we're bonding over our shared love of hip-hop. He's rapping 50 Cent. Too soon, I get the wrap-up signal from the producer, and I end the interview saying, "If you only had more time, I'd take you out on the town and we'd do it right!"

As we took off our microphones, he looked at me and said, "Well, I'm here for two nights, can we go out tonight?"

I thought he was messing with me. His assistant could tell by the look on my face, and said, "He's not joking, he'd like to go out this evening."

Of course I said yes. I was starstruck, but more importantly I was genuinely curious. I felt like I'd gotten a glimpse of the real person, the fun-loving hip-hop fan, behind the imposing illusionist mask. I wanted to get to know that guy.

"Do we have transportation?" he asked me.

I smiled and said, "I've got a 1990 Honda Accord. You can ride shotgun." (I was in my early 20s at the time and yes, I was proud of my ride.) He smiled back and it was on.

He invited me to his show, which totally blew my mind, and then afterward, we drove the Honda Accord to a local lounge in Yaletown, a Vancouver neighborhood full of old warehouses-turned-restaurants. Some local media were curious about the whole setup and came to join the party. We ended up sitting at a big round table, him on my right.

I watched as people threw question after question at him about his celebrity lifestyle. I could hear in his voice that he'd answered those same questions many times before. I started to realize how lonely it might feel, living inside this bubble, where people see you as more of a curiosity than a human being.

I stopped, looked at him, and said: "You have all the fame and fortune any entertainer could wish for. Would you say you're happy as a person?"

He stopped mid-sip of his drink. He put the drink down and stared ahead. I thought to myself, "Damn, I pissed him off." I pictured him standing up and walking out. Evening over.

Then he turned to me and said, "Nobody has really asked me that before." After another short pause, he went on: "I do around 200 shows a year. I'm always on the road. Sometimes I question who my friends are. My relationship just fell apart. I struggle with it."

In that moment, he took his mask off and gave me a glimpse of what his life is really like. He taught me that real connection isn't about perfection. Real connection comes from the ability to embrace imperfection.

The masks we wear

Humans have worn masks almost as long as we've formed societies. Religious rituals in many cultures required masks, as humans impersonated gods, demons, or spirits. From its earliest roots, theater also involved masks, from ancient Greece to Japan's *noh* dramas.

These ancient masks conferred importance on the wearer. Putting a mask on signified a change in which the mask wearer became something larger than themselves—a character, or even a god. But over time, the idea of wearing masks took on negative connotations. In Greek, *hypokrites* literally means "an interpreter from underneath." It was the Greek word for "actor," derived from the idea that actors interpret a play from underneath their masks. Eventually, *hypokrites* became the root of the English word "hypocrite."[1] And mask-wearing became associated with pretending, telling lies, or being (literally) two-faced.

And yet, even before COVID-19 made masks a necessity, we were all wearing multiple masks. We all have multiple roles we play in society—we're workers, we're parents, we're partners, we're friends. In some ways, it's natural to behave a little differently around different people or in different situations. Most of us speak and act a little differently around our parents than we do around our best friends, for example. Neither role is false, but they are different.

Playing these roles can allow us to borrow confidence in moments when we're not sure what we're doing. We mask our insecurities in high-stakes moments. We use masks to conquer our nerves before a big presentation or sales pitch, to overcome the awkwardness when apologizing for a major mistake, to deal with the butterflies when confessing romantic feelings. We take deep breaths; we psych ourselves up; we imitate someone we've seen succeed.

Even in lower-stakes situations, putting on masks can be useful. We put on our "great worker" mask when we go into the office. Athletes put on their "game face" to intimidate the competition. We put on a "poker face" whenever we need to negotiate without "showing our hand" and revealing what really matters. When times get tough, we might put on a "brave face" to support family or friends. Putting on a mask or playing a role can make the people around us more comfortable—if we're all reading from the same social script, we all know what to expect from one another.

In some situations, putting on a mask can actually help you summon the emotion you need to get through a challenging situation. There's a reason "fake it till you make it" is such a popular expression—pretending to be confident can actually boost your confidence, putting on a big smile can actually help you muster more enthusiasm, and maintaining outward calm can help you find true, inner calm.[2] Psychological research proves that "fake it till you make it" can work. Amy Cuddy's TED Talk on so-called "power posing" attracted some controversy, but ultimately the research seems to support her central conclusion: that striking a powerful, open pose can make you feel more confident and powerful.[3]

Living life behind walls

Masks and roles can be beneficial. The feeling of playing a part can help us navigate confusing or stressful situations. But we can't sustain the feeling of faking it for long—eventually, we have a deep need to be seen for who we really are.

Work becomes all the more stressful if you can't be yourself around your colleagues. Relationships can't succeed if you aren't being honest about who you are. It's one thing to laugh at a joke you don't really get, or pretend to like the Smashing Pumpkins to fit in at school (not that I would know what that's like . . .), but if you are hiding deeper, more important parts of yourself, it can be stressful and leave you feeling exhausted and alienated from the people around you.

The term "code-switching" refers to switching between languages, but it can also be used to refer to the way people from minority cultures often have to speak and act like people from the dominant culture to get ahead. Psychologists say there's a real cost to doing that day after day.[4] If you have to think about everything you're saying to make sure you don't slip up and show your real self, you're not truly present in the moment. Your attention is divided; you're constantly scrutinizing yourself, and that's exhausting.

For people in the LGBTQ community who may have had to hide who they are, the damage to both mental and physical health can be severe. Researchers have found that people who've come out to family and friends are less likely to be depressed, and have lower levels of stress hormones, than people who are in the closet. In fact, the opportunity to take down those walls and show the people you care about who you really are is so powerful that the gay and bisexual men in this study who were out actually were less stressed and depressed than the straight men.[5]

Any marriage counselor will tell you that relationships rely on honesty. And many will tell you that one of the common threads among couples who are struggling to remain close is a feeling that one partner has their walls up—that they're not communicating, that they're closed off.[6] A feeling of not being fully heard or seen is incredibly corrosive to an intimate relationship.

"I'd rather be hated for who I am than loved for who I am not." It's unclear who first said these words—many people attribute them to Nirvana front man Kurt Cobain, but there's no real evidence to support that theory. But the message is powerful, wherever it originated. Of course, we all want to be loved. But the feeling of being loved for a persona you're putting on is unsustainable. Ultimately, we all need to be seen for who we really are in order to be healthy and build healthy relationships.

"I'd rather be hated for who I am than loved for who I am not." The Bachelorette star Kaitlyn Bristowe said those words to me in an interview on the TEDxVancouver stage in 2015. The theme of that conference was identity, and I knew Bristowe had some interesting things to say on the topic. But a lot of people felt she didn't deserve to be on that stage. The interview right before we took the stage featured Mohamed Fahmy, an Egyptian Canadian journalist who was wrongfully imprisoned in Egypt. When we walked on stage, I could feel the judgment coming from the audience. Bristowe was just a reality TV star. She wasn't *serious*.

We all need to be
seen for who we really
are in order to be healthy
and **build healthy
relationships**.

————————

But she had the courage to show up, speak out, and be honest. And she changed many minds by doing just that. She said things most *Bachelor* franchise stars won't say: that what we call "reality TV" is more like "manufactured TV." That she went on *The Bachelor* hoping to build a lifestyle brand, not find love. I admired her for speaking her truth, and I know a lot of people in that room (and the hundreds of thousands of people who've watched that interview online) felt the same way. And she's keeping it up—in May 2020, she spoke in a YouTube video about her struggles with depression and addiction before going on *The Bachelor.*[7]

Performing perfection online

Bristowe also shared with me in that interview that she's become a target for cyberbullying. That's an all-too-common experience for people in the public eye. The first time I posted a picture online of me and Lori we were at a Drake concert, and she wanted to post a selfie of the two of us. I think she wanted to know why I hadn't "gone public" with our relationship yet. I warned her that, working in the public eye, any time I post anything online, I'm likely to get some trolls. She said she was ready. Despite an abundance of positive messages from people who were happy to see us happy together, when a troll commented "TOO MUCH PLASTIC SURGERY," I could see she was angry.

Of course she was fired up! It's way too easy for some people to forget that the other people you see posting on social media are also human beings with feelings. Something about the format seems to free people up to say things they'd never say face-to-face. For the record, Lori is a stunner with natural beauty.

Given how toxic social media can be, it's no wonder that most of us tend to have our masks firmly in place when we post on social media. We post carefully curated highlights of our lives. We humblebrag about our greatest accomplishments. We post our most fabulous vacations, our most well-attended parties, our most flattering outfits. We Instagram brunch with friends at that great restaurant, and we don't photograph the bowl of cereal we eat over the sink, alone.

Unfortunately, this tendency to perform perfection can create a vicious cycle. When we see someone else posting from Bali, we feel jealous. And research has shown that we tend to amp up our own perfect posts in response.[8] In other words, when all we see around us are masks of perfection, we feel increasing pressure to keep our own masks on.

It's those moments of comparison that are so toxic for our mental health. Research has been mixed on the psychological effects of social media use overall, but it does seem clear that passively scrolling through a feed composed mainly of people performing perfection is bad for our mental health. Interestingly, one study found that comparing yourself to other people online is linked to depressive symptoms, *even if it's a positive comparison.*[9] Even if your scroll through Facebook leads you to conclude that you're doing better than most of your friends, you're still going to end up more depressed. The very act of comparing ourselves to others is linked to depression.

There's a line in the movie *Election* where the overachieving Tracy Flick says, "Coca-Cola is by far the world's number one soft drink, and they spend more money than anybody on advertising. I guess that's how come they stay number one."[10] Maybe that's what's happening to some of us online—even when we feel like we're coming out on top in the implied who's-the-best competition on Instagram, we still feel the pressure to *stay* number one. By its very nature, perfection demands constant effort. Any single crack in the facade would make you imperfect, destroying all your hard work. Perfectionism is a perfect trap.

When the masks come off

It was the Stanley Cup Finals, Game 7, 2011. The Boston Bruins vs. the Vancouver Canucks, in Vancouver. The Canucks had the chance to win it all for the first time in franchise history, and they lost this crucial game on their home ice.

Walking into the dressing room after this tough loss to interview some of the players was a learning experience to say the least. These guys are like warriors—they never show weakness. Before the game, Vancouver forward Alex Burrows, the team's joker, had been telling me if they won the cup, he'd let me drink from it.

After the game was a different story. These proud men were so raw and vulnerable in their post-game interviews. Goaltender Roberto Luongo and the rest of the players were in tears as they talked about how they'd let the city down. Burrows was nowhere to be seen. The expectations had been through the roof and I could see these players were gutted.

Vancouver hockey fans can be harsh. Later that night there were riots after that loss as randoms came out to capitalize on the chaos and heartbreak. But once the fans saw those interviews, the team won the city back. The players' vulnerability on camera showed fans that they'd wanted a win as badly as we had.

During the early stages of the coronavirus crisis, people worldwide looked to their political leaders for answers. And many leaders stepped up, not just by offering clear information and sensible plans for tackling the problem, but by showing their humanity. In Canada, leaders like British Columbia's Provincial Health Officer, Dr. Bonnie Henry; Ontario Premier Doug Ford; and Manitoba Premier Brian Pallister had tears in their eyes as they addressed the public.

News anchors also showed some vulnerability during this difficult time. CNN anchor Erin Burnett got choked up interviewing a COVID-19 widow. Brian Stelter, host of the Sunday CNN show *Reliable Sources*, received thousands of tweets and emails after he opened up about how he was feeling on the show. "I had tried to bottle it all up," he said. "I guess I was trying to be stoic for my wife and kids. It wasn't until this Friday night that I hit a wall... So my message to you is, when someone asks you if you're OK, right now, tell the truth. It's OK to not be OK." He later told an interviewer that he thought the message had resonated because "People appreciated hearing someone on the other side of the television expressing what they're feeling."[11]

Crying or showing emotion in public has long been taboo, particularly for politicians who are expected to project calm and competence. News anchors, too, have traditionally tried to be stoic even in the face of the most devastating news. In 1963, when President Kennedy was assassinated, Walter Cronkite made the stunning announcement with barely a quaver in his voice. The simple act of taking off his glasses for a moment, the slight hint of emotion in his voice, were memorable precisely because they were so unusual.[12] But by 2020, cultural norms had changed. During a worldwide pandemic, when millions of people were frightened and feeling vulnerable themselves, it was comforting to see leaders show their humanity.

Opening up and showing some real vulnerability can be incredibly powerful for a leader. But it's beneficial for the rest of us, too. Studies find that people tend to believe that, if they showed vulnerability, they'd come across as weak—but when other people show vulnerability, we like them better. In fact, people in a study where participants were asked to sing an improvised song said that the singers appeared strong and brave.[13]

Another study found that people who see colleagues who ask for advice as *more* competent.[14] How many of us are afraid to ask for help? How many of us put pressure on ourselves to know it all and do it all, afraid that others will judge us if we fall short of some imagined goal of perfection? And how many of us worry that admitting we don't know something, or asking for advice, will make people think we're incompetent and can't handle things on our own? The research shows just the opposite: asking for help is a sign of strength. Getting advice from a coworker is a sign that you're *good* at your job.

As Brené Brown has pointed out, the word "courage" comes from the Latin word *cor*, or "heart." Courage originally meant "innermost feelings."[15] Showing your true self to someone else is immensely brave, and at some level we all know that and admire it in other people. It's only ourselves that we hold to this impossible standard of perfection.

Showing vulnerability in our closest relationships is not just beneficial, it's essential. You can't truly know another person unless you know their weaknesses as well as their strengths. And a relationship, whether a friendship or an intimate partnership, can't survive for long if you don't allow the other person to know the real you. Research has actually shown that being around someone who's hiding their true feelings can make your blood pressure rise—not exactly the best foundation for a lasting relationship. Another study found that people who avoided telling even little white lies for a week found that their relationships improved and their social interactions went better.[16]

In close relationships, honesty is like oxygen. And that means being honest about your flaws, your fears, and your insecurities, too.

When vulnerability backfires

Too much information. You probably know the feeling, the way you instinctively draw back when someone overshares. Maybe you know the feeling of oversharing—the flush of embarrassment that comes when you realize that you've said too much.

Vulnerability can be incredibly powerful. It can bring us closer together. But it has the power to damage relationships as well as to strengthen them.

At work, for example, admitting to your flaws can be a great way to make deeper connections with coworkers. But you have to demonstrate your competence first. Otherwise, people will simply dismiss you as too much of a mess to get anything done. That's the conclusion from an interesting study in which participants listened in on an interview where someone was answering trivia questions. If the interviewee had answered most questions correctly, hearing them say they'd spilled coffee on themselves made participants like them more. But if the interviewee hadn't done well on the trivia quiz, participants liked them less after they made a mess.[17]

We like smart, competent people who occasionally spill a little coffee. Maybe that's why it seems like every single rom-com heroine is "clumsy." She's beautiful, smart, funny— and she trips over her own feet! So relatable! So attainable!

But we're turned off by the guy who can't meet his deadlines *and* can't seem to keep his lunch off his shirt. Too much vulnerability—vulnerability in a person who's already demonstrating a lot of weakness—and we smell failure. We turn away.

Excessive vulnerability can backfire if you haven't already demonstrated some of your good qualities. But vulnerability can also backfire if it appears too calculated.

For leaders, for example, showing vulnerability can increase loyalty, engagement, and feelings of connection.[18] But a leader who appears to be reading from a script, or who tries to force a moment of connection, will turn people off. They'll seem inauthentic. Remember, we feel it in our bodies when we're around someone who isn't being truthful. It literally raises our blood pressure. So inauthentic vulnerability—vulnerability put on for show—will have the opposite of the intended effect.

The same is true in interpersonal relationships. If you deliberately share a painful memory with another person because you think it will make them like you more, or get them to agree to do something for you, that person will be able to sense it. And they'll be totally turned off.

As Brené Brown has said, when you try to use vulnerability this way, it's the opposite of taking off your mask. In her book *Daring Greatly*, Brown describes two types of oversharing: "floodlighting," or using emotional information to manipulate, and "the smash and grab," or breaking through someone's boundaries to grab attention for yourself. Both are likely to push people further away from you, not draw them closer.[19]

Why is this kind of calculated sharing so off-putting? Partly, it's because we can sense inauthenticity. But I believe there's something else at work here, too. This kind of manipulative sharing may ping our subconscious alarm bells in part because it shows a lack of regard for our feelings. Research has shown that many psychopaths have high emotional intelligence. They can read other people's emotions easily. But they lack the type of empathy that makes us feel one another's pain. They use their emotional intelligence to manipulate without a qualm.[20] Calculated oversharing is off-putting in part because it shows a bit of that deeply troubling disconnect—an *awareness* of how an emotional story will affect the other person disconnected from any *concern* about that effect. We instinctively recoil from people who appear manipulative, and with good reason.

Of course, oversharing isn't always calculated. We've probably all been in the position of spilling out "word vomit" unintentionally—ranting about something that happened at work even though the person we're talking to isn't all that interested, or spilling all the intimate details of a relationship with an ex to a friend who just casually asked how we were doing. This kind of TMI isn't a deliberate attempt to manipulate, it's just a sign that you're sharing the wrong story at the wrong time.

Sometimes we accidentally overshare because our feelings are too raw. Sometimes we overshare because we desperately need some kind of validation that we haven't been getting in healthier ways. But even when it's unintentional, oversharing can create distance in a moment when you're craving closeness. Wait to talk about fresh wounds until you've processed them a bit on your own, with a therapist, or with an intimate friend. Don't share an emotional story outside of your innermost circle if you still urgently need to be reassured that you're OK, that you're still lovable, that you're a good and valued person.[21] Wait until you have a little distance. And don't share truly personal information with someone you don't know well—sharing needs to be reciprocal to feel comfortable.

How to tell a vulnerable story in a way that engages others

How can we share a piece of ourselves in a way that engages the people we encounter? Good storytelling. Storytelling is one of the most important skills for leading a successful life. If you can tell a great story, you can teach a lesson, inspire commitment and connection, even ace that job interview for your dream gig. Your ability to tell stories is the difference between simply communicating and establishing powerful human connections.

In any presentation, speech, or pivotal conversation, if you want to capture your audience's attention, start with a story. Without exception, the most powerful moment in any interview I've ever done is always a story. That's the moment when the audience leans forward, unwilling to miss a single word. It's the moment when I forget about the cameras and find myself totally engaged with the person I'm interviewing, as if we're alone in the room.

The big challenge, of course, is how to successfully reveal a part of yourself and draw people closer to you. Not every story will do this. A rambling, irrelevant anecdote will make people tune out. An awkward overshare will turn them off. So how do you do this well? How do you actually tell a story about yourself in a way that engages the other person—without oversharing or rambling?

What follows are my five best tips for telling vulnerable stories in a way that draws people in instead of pushing them away.

Clarify your purpose

Before you even begin, ask yourself: "What is the point of this story?" Is your goal to inform, persuade, enlighten, or entertain? Every good story starts with framing a problem that needs solving. Consider this: what does your audience care about right now? Clarify your purpose with a narrative that speaks to their priorities.

Keep in mind that emotion is everything. In memorable interviews, I've consistently seen that the most impactful stories not only were fueled by emotion, but that the best ones had four key ingredients: *hope*, *help*, *heart*, and *humor.* John C. Maxwell outlines these four in one of my favorite books of all time, *Everyone Communicates, Few Connect.*

Briefly, *hope* means telling a story that shows something positive about human nature or offers at least a hint of better things to come; *help* means offering your audience a message they can use in their own lives; *heart* means showing some genuine emotion, or talking about something that truly matters to you; and *humor*, of course, is always welcome.[22] If you have them laughing, you will have them listening (as long as you remember to never make people who are marginalized or less powerful than you the butt of a joke).

If you can deliver one of these things, you'll make an impression. If you deliver all four, your audience will never forget you.

Go first with your truth

Great stories tell the truth in interesting ways. Opening with an unexpected truth or a secret is a great hook off the top, as it creates a sense of intrigue for your listener. Secrets provide motivation—and plot twists—because they may need to be protected or defended. And, let's be honest, everybody is captivated by a powerful personal reveal. If you can, choose a secret with a silver lining, because it sets up a change or transformation.

Read the room, though, and make sure your audience is ready to receive this degree of vulnerability. Remember not to share something that's too fresh, or talk about a painful issue

Your ability to tell stories is the difference between simply communicating and **establishing powerful human connections**.

you haven't yet resolved, unless you're talking to someone you're already in a very close relationship with. Oversharing creates distance, and your goal is to build connection.

Say I started a story by saying, "Last month I received an email I was never supposed to see." Chances are, you're already wondering what that email said. When you begin with the truth or best secret from your story, you'll have your audience asking the most important question: "What happened next?"

Speak to their senses

Our brains absorb stories as if we are experiencing them ourselves. One effective way to tap into this idea is to speak to your audience's senses. When you walked into the room, what did you see, hear, smell, touch, taste? You want the audience to experience your words. These details draw them right into the scene with you. The more detail you can give, the more invested they will become in the plot.

Share your transformation

The best stories deliver a transformational truth. You may have heard that good stories have a beginning, middle, and end. That's what sets them apart from anecdotes. Start with this baseline: hook, development, and climax. Start with something intriguing—like a truth or a secret—develop the theme, and then aim to end on a high note.

If you want to go further and craft a truly authentic story, use this framework: struggle; conflict; resolution.

1   **Struggle.** If people are going to cheer for your success, they need to relate to your struggle first. What did your life look like when you were losing? The realer, the better. Start with the moment when you couldn't pay your bills, when your relationship fell apart, or when you lost your

job. Everyone loves to root for an underdog. Describe the range of emotions behind that struggle and draw the other person in.

2 **Conflict.** What roadblock did you encounter? Really dive into the challenge you were up against. This is your chance to build suspense and set up a cliffhanger. Was it physical conflict, an emotional dilemma—what was at stake?

3 **Resolution.** Until now, your build-up may have created mystery and unpredictability. Your resolution or moment of transformation should be the big reveal. Maybe you saved a life, saved your company from folding, or reconciled with a loved one. Describe the moment where you overcame adversity and explain how this changed you.

The key to this framework is delivering a tangible takeaway, as the entire time, your audience will be asking what's in it for them. Your job is to articulate the lesson learned and give them the meaning behind it. Don't just tell them you met someone new; explain that you learned to value substance over style. Don't just say that you made your sales target; share that you got there by tapping into an unexpected network of contacts. Give them something they can use to be the hero and improve their own lives, and they'll be much more likely to remember your story.

Convey credibility before vulnerability

Getting personal with your storytelling can be a really effective way to connect with someone. But remember, you want to be the competent person who occasionally spills a little coffee, not the total shambles. If you are going to present something raw and personal, make sure you've proven your worth first.

In psychology, this concept is known as the "pratfall effect."[23] How your audience responds to your openness really depends on how they perceive you beforehand. If you have conveyed credibility and strength and then show vulnerability, you will draw people closer. But if people are already questioning your competence, your personal reveal will fall flat, and they may just perceive you as a hot mess.

Earn respect before anything else, and your storytelling skills will help you engage everyone you meet.

Letting go of fear

When I was 22, I was in my final semester at Simon Fraser University, finishing up my bachelor's degree in business and finance. I was on the fast track to a career as an investment broker. This was the mask I thought I had to wear, the role I felt I had to play to please my family and be "successful." Dad would always ask when I was going to get my MBA.

But when I got the chance to facilitate some sessions at a conference in Quebec City, Lotfi, the co-chair of the conference, saw my stage presence and challenged me to pursue a career doing something public-facing. He saw my potential. He said, "You're 22, you have a world of opportunity in front of you."

After reflecting on his belief, "You're right. I'm 22. I'm also from a South Asian family," I told him. "If I don't come home a doctor, lawyer, dentist, or some sort of financial expert, we are going to have a problem here."

Without hesitation, Lotfi fired back, "When are you going to stop playing it safe and start living your life?"

I took my mask off for just a moment and shared the pressure I was facing, and I got a powerful challenge in return to go after something special. From that point on, I started living my life on purpose.

After I graduated, I entered every single contest that might get me closer to a job in media. Local radio sticker spotter contests, internships, whatever I could find. When someone told me that MTV Canada taped a top 10 video countdown show in Vancouver, I went to a taping. I sat in the studio audience. The energy gave me goosebumps, as I watched the host connect through the camera lens. After the taping was over, I took a deep breath, and summoned the courage to walk up to the director and introduce myself. I asked him what it would take for a guy like me to host a show like this.

After giving me the quick once-over, he asked, "What kind of experience do you have?"

None.

"Where did you go to broadcast school?"

I didn't.

"Well," he said, "what can you possibly offer me?"

"An unwavering passion to do this," I said. Silence. Real, long awkward silence. And I waited for an answer.

After what felt like an hour-long pause, the director smiled and told me to come back Friday for a screen test. I had no idea what I was doing, but I believed I had the potential to pursue something great. That was the moment when I began to create a brand-new identity for myself.

In that moment, I learned that the best way to predict the future is to create it for yourself.

We can never control other people's reactions to who we are or what we have to say. All we can control is how we show up. But when you show up as your authentic self, when you're willing to put it all on the line, great things can happen.

It's scary to be vulnerable. We're all afraid of embarrassing ourselves. On a deeper level, we're afraid of judgment.

And that fear isn't trivial. We've evolved over hundreds of thousands of years to be social animals. Rejection is so painful because, deep in our bones, rejection feels like death—because, for our ancestors, rejection from the group *was* a death sentence. Our unconscious minds know that we literally can't survive alone.

But that's the beauty of vulnerability. Because those fears are real, because when you show someone a piece of yourself, you do take a risk, vulnerability retains its power. But if we all walk around with our metaphorical masks on, we can't truly know one another. We can't connect.

So take that risk. Go first. Take off your mask and try to make a connection. The people in your life will thank you.

4

BE ASSERTIVELY EMPATHETIC

"Going high" doesn't mean you're not angry, but it does mean that you retain your empathy. **How often are we failing to live up to that high standard?**

A BLACK MAN asked a white woman to put her dog on a leash. That's how the incident in Central Park began. As Christian Cooper, a Black man who loves bird-watching, began filming the white woman, Amy Cooper, she called 911 and claimed that "an African American man" was "threatening" her. In the video, you can hear her voice trembling in a way that it wasn't just moments before. It's hard not to draw the conclusion that she's performing fear in order to make herself out to be a victim.

When the video went viral, Amy Cooper was fired from her job. For many people, this video brought up a long, dark history of white people calling the police on Black people while they were simply going about their daily lives. And worse. As Christian Cooper put it in an interview with the *New York Times*, "There are certain dark societal impulses that she, as a white woman facing in a conflict with a Black man, that she thought she could marshal to her advantage."

And yet, in interviews after the incident, Christian Cooper expressed concern for Amy Cooper and how her life had been changed by this incident. "Any of us can make—not necessarily a racist mistake, but a mistake," he told the *New York Times*. "And to get that kind of tidal wave in such a compressed period of time, it's got to hurt. It's got to hurt... I'm not excusing the racism. But I don't know if her life needed to be torn apart."

To NPR, he said, "I'm not sure that her one minute of poor decision-making, bad judgment and, without question, racist response necessarily has to define her completely."[1]

To CNN, he said that he thought her apology, released shortly after the incident, had been sincere, although he wasn't certain that she had fully realized that her actions had been racist. He also said: "I find it strange that people who were upset that... that she tried to bring death by cop down on my head, would then turn around and try to put death threats on her head. Where is the logic in that? Where does that make any kind of sense?"

I'm moved by the empathy I hear Christian Cooper expressing in those comments. He's not shying away from calling Amy Cooper's actions what they were: racist. But he's also refusing to define her as a person by her actions on one day. He's putting himself in her shoes, even though she failed to do the same for him, and thinking about how she must be hurting as she loses her job and faces widespread condemnation and even death threats online.

Michelle Obama said, "When they go low, we go high." And that's exactly what Christian Cooper has done. "Going high" doesn't mean you're not angry; it doesn't mean you excuse bad or dangerous behavior; it doesn't even mean that you are required to forgive someone who has hurt you. But it does mean that, like Christian Cooper, you stay focused on your long-term goals, and you retain your empathy.[2]

How often are we failing to live up to that high standard?

Empathy is on the decline

"Going low" seems to be more common than ever in today's world. Everywhere you look, you can see politicians viciously attacking each other and ordinary people calling each other morons and worse online. And it's not just that we perceive we're living through a more polarized, less empathetic time. Research actually backs that impression up: in 2009, the average American college student was less empathetic than most students in 1979.[3]

Jamil Zaki, the author of the book *The War for Kindness*, argues that while humans evolved the ability to empathize as an adaptive trait that allows us to cooperate and live together in groups, the way we live now works to undermine our natural empathetic abilities.[4]

Basically, we evolved to live in *small* groups. Our ancient ancestors knew everyone they hunted and gathered with. Their relationships with their tribes were long term and reciprocal. But today, we're more and more likely to live crowded together in urban environments with a lot of people we don't actually know. We have more fleeting interactions with people we aren't in relationship with. And, as we discussed in Part One, we spend less and less time in ongoing communities like religious organizations, labor unions, and even bowling leagues. The people we're closest to are as likely to be 1,000 miles away as they are to be right next door.

We also spend more of our time online. And while social media didn't cause the fracturing of communal spaces, it is almost perfectly designed to undermine empathy. There are a number of factors that make it easier to attack and insult people online. Anonymity is one. Experts believe that the inability to see other people and gauge their reactions is another.[5] Even the relative newness of social media, and the resulting lack of established social norms, may play a role. Sitting behind a screen, invisible to the person you're insulting and unable to see the pain on their face, in a virtual space that feels lawless—and consequence-free—is basically a perfect storm of factors that work to rob us of our ability to see things through another person's eyes.

It's no secret that social media is particularly toxic for women, people of color, and members of the LGBTQ community. Amnesty International ran a year-long study of 778 female politicians and journalists and found that a "problematic" or "abusive" tweet was sent to one of the women in the study every 30 seconds.[6] The problem was particularly acute for women of color, who were 34% more likely to receive online abuse than white women, and worse for Black women in particular, who were 84% more likely than white women to receive abusive tweets. And in a survey by Galop, a U.K.-based LGBTQ anti-violence charity, 80% of respondents had experienced anti-LGBTQ hate speech online, with trans people more likely to receive abuse than cisgender people.

Hate speech and hate crimes have been on the rise in real life, too. In 2018, hate crimes reached a 16-year high in America, according to the FBI.[7] Hate crimes and incidents of racism against Asian Americans spiked during the coronavirus crisis. One professor documented almost 2,000 incidents in just two months. We saw similar problems in Canada. In Vancouver, police identified 77 hate-associated incidents in the first five months of 2020, and opened 29 investigations specifically into anti-Asian crime during that time, compared to only 4 such incidents in the first five months of 2019. The leaders behind the #HealthNotHate campaign encouraged people to speak out against racism and to keep the focus on defeating the virus, not attacking each other.[8]

The coronavirus compounded our society's ongoing crisis of empathy. In the United States, people of color were much more likely to die from the disease than white people, for a host of reasons, including unequal access to health care and greater concentration in low-paid yet high-risk occupations that precluded social distancing. People experiencing homelessness were also at high risk. One study estimated that homeless people would be two to four times more likely to be hospitalized due to the virus.[9]

The coronavirus didn't create the deep inequalities in our society. It didn't make us fail to empathize for people who are different from us. But it did make that failure impossible to ignore.

Similarly, when Derek Chauvin was charged with George Floyd's murder, it was far (very far) from the first time that an unarmed Black person in America died at the hands of police. But the video of Floyd's death went viral at a time when Black Americans were already feeling the unequal impact of both the coronavirus itself and of the recession it caused. The Black Lives Matter protests that followed were, according to historians, the biggest mass movement in American history, with 15 to 26 million people protesting. And the movement wasn't just American: people marched and protested around the world, from London to Seoul to Sydney to Idlib, Syria. Lori, Nico, and I went to a powerful protest here in Vancouver.

The Black Lives Matter movement had been around for years by the time of George Floyd's murder. But in 2020, something was different. Many more people, in many more places, were coming out to show their support for the movement. According to an analysis by the *New York Times*, there were protests in more than 40% of the counties in the United States, and almost 95% of the counties that held protests were majority white.[10]

Something about the moment made George Floyd's death impossible to ignore. Something about the moment made empathy possible. And that empathy began to spark real change.

The difference empathy makes: a tale of two countries

Many people in North America responded to the coronavirus with an outpouring of love and concern for their fellow human beings. Doctors, nurses, and other medical staff showed enormous courage. They put themselves in harm's way to care for people who were sick and suffering.

Millions of Americans, like people around the world, responded quickly to the call to stay home and help slow the spread of the virus. In fact, most people started staying home before they were required to do so by state-mandated lockdown orders.[11] Told that doctors and nurses were suffering from a shortage of personal protective equipment, thousands of people started sewing cloth masks at home to donate to hospitals.[12]

I believe what people around the world craved most from their leaders when the coronavirus hit was empathy. Leaders guided by empathy didn't sugarcoat what was happening, but they did acknowledge the fear everyone was feeling. Like Dr. Bonnie Henry, the Provincial Health Officer for British Columbia. She was the one who announced our province's lockdowns, and she ended her announcement with a line she ended up repeating often: "This is our time to be kind, to be calm, and to be safe."

Dr. Henry consistently showed empathy throughout the crisis. She teared up when she had to announce that there were coronavirus cases in our long-term care homes. She

The pandemic didn't make us fail to empathize for people who are different from us. **But it did make that failure impossible to ignore**.

refused to push police to enforce social distancing in public spaces and during protests, to avoid traumatizing people who were already struggling. And she got results: British Columbia was able to start safely reopening in June 2020, at a time when other provinces were still struggling to control outbreaks.[13]

Unfortunately for our neighbors to the south, President Donald Trump showed no such empathy as the first wave of the coronavirus rolled across the country, with devastating effects. He didn't meet with survivors or families who'd lost loved ones to the pandemic. He didn't even publicly express any sadness for the thousands of deaths. And when former president George W. Bush released a video message calling for Americans to come together in a "spirit of service and sacrifice," Trump complained that Bush hadn't come to his defense during his impeachment.[14]

That lack of empathy at the top had serious consequences for ordinary Americans. Throughout the early phases of the crisis, Trump focused more on the economy and the headlines of the day than on managing the public health response.[15] His lack of empathy for other people and continued focus on how the crisis would affect *him* and his reelection campaign left the federal government scrambling to manage the crisis.

Contrast Trump's brash, combative style with New Zealand prime minister Jacinda Ardern's calm, empathetic leadership. The two leaders couldn't be more different—and their two countries' experiences with the virus have been starkly different as well. Of course, empathy wasn't Ardern's only strength, but it played a significant role in making her both more effective and more popular during the early phase of the crisis.

Ardern moved quickly to impose a very strict lockdown. She didn't sugarcoat her message: she was clear from the beginning that this would be a difficult period for New

Zealand. But she coupled her strict guidelines with clear moments of empathy. She appeared regularly on Facebook Live, answering people's questions, giving viewers glimpses of her home life, and putting a human face on strict policies by talking about the "loud honk" of the emergency alert system or explaining why playgrounds were off limits. She announced that she and other top government officials would be taking a 20% pay cut for six months. And she ended every public address with the same simple message: "Be strong. Be kind."[16]

By mid-May 2020, New Zealand was moving to reopen businesses—after losing only 12 souls to the coronavirus.[17] At the same time, America was pushing to reopen businesses, too—even as the coronavirus continued to spread in many places, and after losing more Americans than were killed in the Vietnam War.[18] A majority of Americans disapproved of Trump's handling of the crisis.[19] Ardern was her country's most popular leader in a century.[20]

The power of empathy online

During the coronavirus crisis, many of us stayed home and interacted with the world primarily through screens. We watched the news, we video-chatted with friends and coworkers, and we spent endless hours scrolling through social media.

It was easy to find examples of anger and fear online. Some people were posting about how angry they were about lockdowns. Some were posting about how angry they were about people protesting lockdowns. People were shaming each other for not wearing masks and arguing about the effectiveness of vaccines.

But it was also pretty easy to find examples of people reaching out, connecting, sharing their feelings, and being empathetic toward those who were suffering. Social media showed us the best of humanity, not just the worst.

Some theorists have argued that the largest social media platforms are designed to undermine empathy. Facebook and Twitter thrive by keeping us online, and outrage seems to encourage people to share, drawing more eyeballs to content and keeping us all heads-down in the virtual world. But if social media is designed to make us angry and fearful, that suggests it could be redesigned to foster different emotions. Some developers have actually purpose-built online communities that reward changing someone's mind on a topic or encourage sharing and mutual support.[21] These communities actually *encourage* empathy.

Even within the big social media platforms we already have, which aren't built to reward empathy, you can deliberately practice empathy. You can choose to use social media as a tool to connect rather than a place to loudly proclaim your opinions, compare yourself to other people, or pick fights. One simple thing I do is, when I have the impulse to "like" something a friend has posted, I push myself to take just one more moment and write a comment, too. That way, instead of just boosting my friend's statistics, I'm actually engaging with them. Other experts have suggested deliberately using social media to expose yourself to people from other parts of the world or different walks of life. Even something as simple as taking a deep breath before you post a comment can help you move out of fear, anger, or defensiveness and into empathy.[22]

Sarah Silverman, once famous for shock comedy that sometimes involved racist slurs, went viral a couple of years ago for reaching out to a Twitter troll. He tweeted an unprintable word at her, and instead of cursing him out or even just ignoring him, she got curious. She clicked through to his timeline and saw he'd mentioned dealing with severe back pain. She replied, "I see what ur doing & your rage is thinly veiled pain. But u know that. I know this feeling. Ps My back... sux too. see what happens when u choose love."

By reaching out and showing him some empathy, Silverman unlocked something in a guy who'd previously spent most of his time online tweeting racial slurs. He responded by sharing that he couldn't choose love because he'd been abused when he was just eight years old. Silverman encouraged him to seek out a support group and asked her followers to help him raise money and find a doctor to help him deal with his back pain.

Months later, they were still exchanging direct messages on Twitter every day.[23] The troll and his victim had become friends.

Our culture of avoidance

Sarah Silverman did something pretty extraordinary with that Twitter troll. When a conflict began, she moved toward it instead of backing away. She engaged—she got curious—she tried to learn more about the perspective of the person who was attacking her.

Most of us would do the opposite.

Surveys consistently show that the majority of people avoid tough conversations. In one survey, 25% of people said they'd been putting off a difficult conversation for at least six months. In another, half of respondents said they had avoided someone they needed to have a tough talk with, in some cases for as long as *two years*. Another survey found that 70% of people were currently avoiding a difficult conversation, and 53% were dealing with "toxic" workplace dynamics by ignoring them.[24]

The problem of avoidance is particularly bad at the smallest and largest companies.[25] At big organizations, HR may seem like a distant, faceless department. Some people might not know who their HR rep is, making it hard to approach them with a delicate issue. People at small companies, conversely, have the exact opposite problem: they know their coworkers *too* well. They're afraid of upsetting the balance of those necessarily close relationships.

A culture of avoidance can have serious consequences. One study focused on health care providers in oncology departments found that even in this high-stakes environment, nurses often avoided talking about ethical concerns until there was some kind of crisis that forced them to address the issue. The researchers found several reasons people avoided these conversations, including the feeling that dealing with these complicated issues was emotionally draining, the emphasis on efficiency at work, and a fear that bringing up ethical concerns would damage their relationships.[26]

In a healthy work culture, people are able and even encouraged to speak up about ethical concerns. One analysis of corporations that had internal reporting systems for ethical questions found that the companies that saw *more* reports to those internal hotlines actually ended up with *fewer* external issues like lawsuits.[27] Creating a culture where people are willing to speak up about difficult issues allows problems to be resolved earlier—before they turn into serious crises. Too bad that so many of us avoid tough conversations at work.

And it's not just at work. Take dating: as many as 80% of Millennials say they've been ghosted by someone they dated.[28] "Ghosting," if you're not familiar, means that instead of simply telling another human being you've spent quality time with that you no longer want to date them, you just... never contact them again. It's the coward's way out of a relationship, and it's alarmingly common.

Relationship experts say that avoiding difficult conversations with a partner is actually a sign that you should break up.[29] (Hopefully not by ghosting.) If there are things you feel you can't say to your partner, or questions you're too afraid to ask, then the relationship itself is in trouble. I'd say the same is true for close friends—if a friend says or does something that upsets you, and you avoid confronting the issue, you will inevitably start to drift apart. Closeness of any kind requires communication, and at some point that's going to mean confrontation.

One of the top five regrets expressed by people on their deathbeds is "I wish I'd had the courage to express my feelings."[30] According to palliative care nurse Bronnie Ware, the author of the book *The Top Five Regrets of the Dying*, people who avoid talking about their feelings to keep the peace with friends and family can even become physically ill as a result of holding on to resentment. Avoiding difficult conversations can literally make us sick—and we will, ultimately, regret it.

Strategies for building empathy

OK, you're convinced. You need to learn how to have difficult conversations. Where do you start?

Start with empathy. If you enter a tough conversation with the intention of doing your best to understand where the other person is coming from, hearing what they have to say, and respecting their feelings, you have a much better chance of getting to a successful outcome—whether that means repairing a relationship, dealing with an ethical issue, correcting a mistake, or getting back the money you loaned to a friend. Here are some strategies that can help you increase your own empathy:

Practice. The first strategy is the simplest: take some time to practice putting yourself in someone else's shoes. You can do this as an exercise any time. Take a few minutes to imagine how someone you know might be feeling right now.[31] If they're in a bad mood, what might have set it off? How would you feel if you were dealing with the problem they're facing? What do you know about their hopes, fears, and goals that would help you imagine what they're feeling?

Push yourself. Don't just put yourself in the shoes of a friend or close colleague. Challenge yourself to imagine the perspective of someone who's really different from you.[32] Think about someone you know who has different political beliefs than you do. Can you imagine how they might have come to those beliefs, or why that cause is so important to them?

Read fiction. Researchers have found that reading fiction improves what psychologists call "theory of mind," or the ability to understand another person's emotional state.[33] Reading a novel drops you into a character's mind and lets you see the world through another set of eyes. Bonus points if you read a novel written by and about a person who's different from you.

Reflect on your biases. We all have unconscious biases and prejudices that might keep us from empathizing from people who are different from us. The first step to bringing down those barriers to empathy is to recognize that they exist. Project Implicit, at Harvard, offers a series of tests that can help you uncover some of your own biases.[34]

Focus on similarities. If you're struggling to find empathy for someone in your life, try focusing on what you have in common.[35] Are you both parents? Do you both like dogs? Something as simple as "We both want this company we work for to succeed" could be a starting place that helps you begin to assume positive intentions on their part.

Put yourself in someone else's shoes. During the May 2020 protests following the police killing of George Floyd, Genesee County Sheriff Chris Swanson put down his helmet and baton and spoke to protestors in Flint, Michigan. When they started chanting, "Walk with us," he did just that.[36] What can you do to walk a mile in someone else's shoes? Can you try out a different house of worship than one you might normally attend? Think of an event you would never go to and give it a try. See if it helps you see the world from a different perspective.

Practice small acts of kindness. Sometimes you have to fake it till you make it. When dealing with someone you dislike, the simple act of saying something nice to them can actually help you develop warmer feelings toward them.[37] Take a deep breath, smile, and tell them you like their shirt, or ask how their weekend was. See if that changes the way you feel.

How to have difficult conversations

I interviewed the great Salman Rushdie after the publication of his novel *The Golden House*. Rushdie has found himself in the center of difficult cultural conversations ever since Ayatollah Khomeini of Iran issued a fatwa, or religious decree, calling for Muslims to kill Rushdie because his novel *The Satanic Verses* was, according to Khomeini, blasphemous.[38]

I asked Rushdie how we get people to productively disagree in a polarized time. "Well," he said, "we used to be able to do it." He argued that we just need to rediscover the ability to disagree without piling on and shaming people or shouting them down for saying something we dislike. "We've all got to grow up a little bit," he said.

It does take some emotional maturity to disagree productively. In their book *Crucial Conversations: Tools for Talking When Stakes Are High*, authors Kerry Patterson, Joseph Grenny, Ron McMillan, and Al Switzler define crucial conversations as ones where there are opposing opinions, strong emotions, and high stakes. They share a few examples, including asking a roommate to move out, confronting a loved one about substance abuse, delivering negative feedback at work, or talking to a colleague who's made offensive comments.

In every one of those situations, and many more high-stakes, emotionally tricky conversations, getting to a successful outcome without damaging the relationship beyond repair takes courage, emotional intelligence, and empathy. But the good news is you don't have to be the Dalai Lama to succeed in these kinds of situations. With a little practice confronting difficult issues, you can learn to handle these crucial conversations more successfully.

Here are my five best tips for navigating difficult conversations.

Be assertively empathetic

When we're relaying bad news, it's easy to fall into the trap of getting caught up in our own experience and focusing on how difficult it is to share tough news, or how scary it might be for us to witness an emotional reaction. But we have to push past this.

If you have to say something difficult, do your best to identify with their experience, not just your own. While you've been carrying around the burden of deciding when and how you will drop your truth bomb, the impact is a fresh wound for the other side.

Consider framing the approach like this: *relationship first, logic second.* Relationships are the foundation for productive conversation. Start by acknowledging their concern. They might have an intense emotional reaction. Just listen. Maybe they say nothing. Just listen. The silence can be profound. If the silence persists, then lean in with follow-up questions without placing blame. For example, "Tell me about what you're struggling with." Keep it neutral. Don't make assumptions about what they're feeling—be open to anything they might have to say.

If they have questions for you, make sure you understand what they are asking and acknowledge their concern. "Can you elaborate on that?" "Can you help me better understand your question?"

Cultivating authentic curiosity beforehand will help you anticipate the other side's concerns. Consider their personal reality, job or business prospects, any major life events they're dealing with. This form of assertive empathy will show respect, allow you to answer their questions thoughtfully, and help de-escalate conflict.

Remember, anything you say after your reveal may very well be forgotten, as their mind is focused on processing the news you just shared. Deliver your news and then focus on their response. People want to be seen, heard, and respected. Allow them to do just that and stop talking.

Keep in mind, difficult conversations rarely go as planned. The best thing you can do is lead with assertive empathy and just listen.

Difficult conversations can be uncomfortable. **Avoiding them is worse**.

Know that they *can* handle the truth

Research from Brigham Young University proved that when it comes to receiving bad news, most people prefer directness over an attempt to ease the pain with a drawn-out "softball" opening.[39] This finding was particularly strong in cases where the bad news involved some kind of social relationship. Think "I want to break up," or "You're fired."

Introduce a quick buffer phrase like "Can we talk?" to give the other person a few seconds to process that some tough news is coming. Greet them respectfully, and then get straight to the point. Drawing bad news out, or trying to soften it with euphemisms, is something we do to protect ourselves as the messengers for bad news. But when we're on the receiving end, we always want to hear the tough truth in a simple and straightforward manner.

Let go of likability

This one will be tough for the people-pleasers out there. Difficult conversations can be uncomfortable. Avoiding them is worse. Even if you come into the conversation with respect and a positive intent, research published in the *Harvard Business Review* proves when we receive bad news, we blame the messenger. Even with relatively low stakes, we dislike people who give us bad news.[40]

Lucky you.

We all have a powerful need to make sense of the events happening to us. And a key part of creating an explanation of an unexpected experience is assigning blame. But leadership isn't about comfort, it's about effective action. Managing this expectation of likability will help you avoid taking things personally and keep you focused on the end goal of your conversation.

Even in a social context, if your goal—ending a relationship respectfully, confronting a serious behavior problem, recovering money you loaned someone—is important enough, you owe it to yourself and to the other person to take the hit and confront the situation directly. They won't like it, but it has to be done. And in the long run, behaving honestly and with empathy will lead to a stronger relationship than brushing serious issues under the rug.

Own your emotions

You can't control anyone else's emotions. But you can own your own. When things get heated, it's easy to throw out words that you can't take back: "You always _____." "You never _____." These kinds of broad generalizations will get in the way of achieving any kind of productive outcome. And let's not forget the two most dangerous words in the English language, the words that will turn any difficult conversation into a dumpster fire: "Calm down."

How do you get a handle on your emotions? A 2013 study by researchers at the University of Minnesota looked at how to create a safe space when getting into an argument. One key finding was the importance of "I" statements.[41] Consider this when you're getting worked up: instead of saying "You're making me crazy" or "Don't raise your voice to me," stick to acknowledging your own feelings:

- "I'm feeling angry."
- "I'm feeling frustrated."
- "I'm feeling defeated."

Never say "You make me feel" anything. Once you get into the blame game, you create a hostile dynamic.

Let's be real, if you are sharing bad news, you're most likely going to get a heightened emotional response. Don't try to talk them out of being bothered. Own your emotions and just listen. If you give them respect, chances are you will get it back in return.

Focus on what you can agree on

Before I got married years ago, a friend gave me a great piece of relationship advice: "Do you want to be right or be in a relationship?" To this day, it's a powerful reminder of how to approach any difficult conversation. For the record, Lori is a lawyer, so I'll stick with being in the relationship.

There is always common ground. Find it by working through their responses: "What's the real challenge?" "What would it take for this to work for you?" "What does your ideal scenario look like?" Once you hear their concerns, start finding ways to improve the process, project, or personal relationship and do it together.

People want to feel a sense of belonging. If you can lead with the truth, acknowledge their concern, and be assertively empathetic, the difficult conversation can help you both conquer the conflict in front of you.

Relationship first, logic second

The core principle to remember in any difficult conversation is to focus on the relationship first and logic second. Your goal should never be to "win." You're not there to score points or come up with devastatingly witty comebacks. You're there to communicate your news, whatever it is, hear and accept their response—whatever it is—and leave with your dignity intact.

Your goal should be to preserve the relationship. If you get into a political discussion with someone you disagree with, focus on trying to listen and understand their point of view. It's more respectful than just spouting off your own talking points—and, incidentally, it's also more likely to get them to change their mind.[42] If you have to broach a tough topic at work, remember that you're going to continue working with this person. And even if you won't be working with them because you're letting them go, in most cases you probably want to keep them as a professional contact and someone who will speak well of you and the company. Even in a breakup conversation, where you're completely terminating a relationship, you want to leave the room with your head held high—right?

When in doubt, just stop talking. That's the advice Dr. John Gray, the author of the classic book *Men Are from Mars, Women Are from Venus*, gave me when I interviewed him on BTV. He explained that, when you get into conflict, you can trigger your fight-or-flight response, and that stops the blood flow to the thinking parts of your brain. That's the worst thing that can happen in a tough conversation. You need all your wits about you to get through a conflict without losing your cool.

So if you feel yourself getting drawn out of your ideal, empathetic state, just stop talking. Listen. Reorient yourself toward the other person and what they're experiencing and you'll end up making them feel valuable instead of like a villain.

Don't let discomfort hold you back

Social media can be a toxic space for marginalized people. But social media has also created new spaces where people can speak truth to power. Every so often, something good goes viral.

Take the hashtag #MeAndWhiteSupremacy. Started by an activist named Layla F. Saad, it's an online movement that encourages white women to examine their own privilege and their own internalized racism. Saad first created a 28-day Instagram challenge, but when the challenge went viral, she created a workbook with exercises that prompt people to reflect on their own complicity in white supremacist systems.

Reflecting on your own privilege can be uncomfortable. Most white people prefer to think of racism as something that only "bad" people perpetuate. It's hard to reconcile your sense of yourself as a good person with the idea that you benefit from racist systems. But, as Saad told *Elle* magazine, that's exactly the point: "To have a productive conversation about race and white supremacy, one must find ways to be at ease in discomfort, or at least invite discomfort in and sit with it."[43]

Empathy isn't always easy. It isn't always comfortable. Too often, the easiest thing to do is to retreat to our corners and tell ourselves that we are right and the person disagreeing with us is wrong—and probably stupid. And mean. But holding on to our own perspective too tightly can hold us back from connecting.

Don't let discomfort hold you back from making a real connection. When you encounter a perspective that's different from yours, sit with that discomfort. Get curious. Own your own emotions and remain open to the other person's emotions. Be assertively empathetic. You could change someone's life—or the world.

5

MAKE PEOPLE FEEL FAMOUS

If you make an effort to lift people up, you'll connect with them on a very genuine, human level. **And they'll remember you for it**.

MOM AND I were watching the news together after she got home from work. I was seven. There was a segment about Rick Hansen. She told me, "Watch this man. He's making a difference in the world. This is what leading and giving is all about."

In 1973, when he was just 15 years old, Rick was thrown out of the back of a pickup truck and paralyzed from the waist down. He went on to become a Paralympic athlete, and started a foundation devoted to funding research and building a more inclusive world.

When Mom and I saw him on television, Rick was in the middle of his Man in Motion World Tour, traveling all the way around the world in his wheelchair to show what people with disabilities can really do, highlight the need for more inclusive spaces, and raise money for spinal cord research. That 26-month journey ultimately raised $26 million—and he hasn't stopped since.[1]

Those conversations with Mom stuck with me. I have had several opportunities to interview Rick over the years. Any time he enters a room, you can feel the energy shift. Whoever he is talking to, he always leans in and makes the conversation all about the other person. His curiosity is contagious. He's an immensely warm person, and I've always been inspired by how relentless he is in his drive to create a world of accessibility for all.

In 2012, Rick and his team wanted to do something special to mark the 25th anniversary of the Man in Motion tour. They decided to recreate a part of the journey by traveling across Canada, honoring difference makers. For the final day of this tour, they reached out to *Breakfast Television* to ask for a volunteer to participate and run a short leg of the relay along with Rick. I was thrilled to be chosen.

When Rick knew it would be me, his team then asked if I wanted to hand off the relay medal to Mom when I had completed my portion of the race. Twenty-five years later, Rick remembered that Mom had worked in the accounting department on the original tour team. Not only did he remember, he was thoughtful enough to create this milestone moment for the two of us.

Running beside Rick down Hastings Street in Vancouver that morning, I could see all the people lining up to salute him for everything he'd accomplished. I was proud to be by his side.

When it came time to hand off the medal to Mom, Rick said, "Wait." He raised her arm like a champion. It felt like she was on the podium receiving a medal. I'd never seen her smile so bright. The older I get, the more I realize the sacrifices both Mom and Dad made for our family. To see her star get to shine that way brought tears to my eyes.

That morning, Mom had brought her Man in Motion tour book from the '80s. Still in mint condition. It had photos of the team inside. When Rick opened it up, he could identify all of the people on the team.

I looked at him and said, "Rick, how could you possibly remember all of these people?"

He said, "Everybody wants to be appreciated. If you can find creative ways to make people feel valuable, you will cultivate a culture of loyalty in your life."

The spirit of gratitude

Rick Hansen is an inspiring leader in so many ways. But for me, the way he makes the effort to remember people and recognize their hard work stands out. I will never forget the moment he created for me and Mom. A lesser man might have turned that 25th anniversary tour into a victory lap for himself. After all, he did accomplish something truly remarkable. But Rick used that tour to recognize all the people, like Mom, who had helped him along the way. He led with gratitude, and I will never forget it.

There are many ways to bring a spirit of gratitude into our relationships. Here's how I think about it: I strive to *make people feel famous.* Just like Rick Hansen did with me and Mom, I look for opportunities to shine a spotlight on someone else. Even if it's just for a moment—a simple "thank you," a few words of gratitude, or a brief recognition of something they've done—if you make an effort to lift people up, you'll connect with them on a very genuine, human level. And they'll remember you for it.

Gratitude is even more important in times of crisis. As Rebecca Solnit has so eloquently written, most notably in her book *A Paradise Built in Hell*, most people's first instinct in a crisis is to reach out and help someone: "we survive by coming together." But Solnit also points out that in order to sustain this kind of altruism, we need to believe that other people will also step up. If we believe that most people are selfish and are only looking out for themselves, we'll end up feeling like reaching out a hand to a fellow human being in need is too much of a risk.[2]

That's one reason gratitude is so important. Taking a moment to recognize that beautiful human impulse to help is itself a way to help, by reminding everyone—yourself included—that we all have the potential to do good in the world.

Gratitude is also crucial in a crisis because crisis takes so much out of us. In a true disaster, first responders may suffer from post-traumatic stress disorder for years afterward. Even people who are a step removed from trauma, like therapists, journalists, and lawyers, can end up with PTSD simply because they've stepped up to help others process and deal with traumatic events.[3] Taking a moment to express gratitude can create a moment of calm and even optimism in the midst of darkness.[4]

It may never be possible to fully assess the toll that dealing with the coronavirus crisis will take on nurses and other health care workers. But we know that hundreds of thousands of nurses stepped up in truly heroic ways to care for their neighbors, despite the risk to their own health, and the need to isolate from their families to avoid spreading the virus. One nurse from Minnesota, Shareen Parashakallah (along with three friends and fellow nurses) actually left her home to go to New York to help where the crisis was most severe during the early stages. Another nurse whose wedding had to be postponed due to social distancing guidelines ended up getting married in a hospital break room—with the groom dialing in via FaceTime.[5]

Seeing the enormous sacrifices nurses have made, millions of people around the world have responded with an outpouring of gratitude. Here in Vancouver, British Columbia, the 7 p.m. cheer brought a community together to celebrate our front-line heroes. In the United States, that same gesture in New York City[6] is probably the most well-known example. But the phenomenon is actually worldwide, and seems to have started in Wuhan, the very epicenter of the virus.[7]

Gratitude and appreciation for health care workers also spread online and on social media. One nursing website compiled words of gratitude for nurses from people around the world:

"There are no words to describe how brave you are and how grateful I am...."

"We could not be more thankful of the work that you do every single day, fearlessly serving others without putting yourself first...."

"Thank you for your tireless efforts and for sharing your gifts with others. We notice you, we appreciate you, we thank you."[8]

One lucky nurse got a more tangible expression of gratitude: a $10,000 Postmates gift card from Jennifer Aniston. After appearing on *Jimmy Kimmel Live from His House* in April 2020, Aniston surprised nurse Kimball Fairbanks with some words of gratitude and this unexpected gift. Postmates also gave Fairbanks' coworkers on her floor gift cards of their own.[9] For Jennifer Aniston to use the power of her celebrity to turn the spotlight on an ordinary nurse stepping up to do extraordinary work—talk about making people feel famous!

The anonymous street artist known as Banksy surprised nurses and staff at Southampton General Hospital in England with a new artwork celebrating their hard work. The piece shows a boy playing with a superhero nurse doll, his old Batman and Superman toys tossed aside. The artist also left a note that read, "Thanks for all you're doing. I hope this brightens the place up a bit, even if it's only black and white."[10]

Many companies also shared messages of gratitude for nurses and other front-line workers who stepped up during the coronavirus crisis. In Canada, General Mills honored five food bank workers by putting their faces on Cheerios boxes along with the words "Food Bank Hero." One of them was my cousin Feezah Jaffer, the executive director of the Surrey Food Bank.

I have to brag on Feezah for a second and share that she used the opportunity of being recognized for her amazing work to turn the spotlight on her staff and volunteers: "It's amazing, really humbling to be chosen. Mostly because it highlights the work that all of our staff and volunteers are doing. Without them nothing would happen; they're really the front-line heroes."[11]

That's real leadership.

Generous leadership

Leading with gratitude is enormously powerful. Recognizing others for their hard work is a powerful way to motivate and engage them. In the workplace, gratitude and recognition can be the difference between an engaged and inspired culture and an office full of people going through the motions. Research from Gallup has shown that the companies with the highest levels of employee engagement tend to motivate their employees with praise. When people get recognition at least once a week, they're more productive, they stay with the organization longer, and they get better customer-satisfaction scores. Another survey found that feeling encouraged and recognized for their work was one of the top five things that motivated people to work hard. In fact, while 37% of people say they work harder if they're afraid they might lose their job, 81% say they work harder when they get some appreciation from the boss.[12] It's simple: praising people makes them work harder and do better.

Think back on the bosses you've had in your own career. I bet you remember the ones who took the time to call out the

Leading with
gratitude is enormously
powerful. Take the
opportunity to **praise
others to remind
them *why* their work
is so important**.

---

hard work you were doing or recognize your contributions to big projects. I bet they inspired you to do your best. And I bet you loved working for them.

Of course, most workplaces don't go through the kind of intense crises that nurses, grocery store workers, and delivery workers suffered during the pandemic. But long-term, low-grade stress also takes its toll on the mind and body. Even if the "crisis" is simply finishing a major project, hitting a big quarterly goal, or working long hours to make a tight deadline, a little bit of appreciation goes a long way.

There are a lot of ways leaders can show appreciation, from the always-welcome pay raise to an unexpected reward, a public shout-out, or a quick thank-you note.[13] Not all praise is created equal, however. Leaders, parents, teachers, and others who want to motivate through praise should focus on a few key principles of effective praise:[14]

- **Praise should be specific.** "Great job on that project" is nice to hear, but "I really appreciated the way you took the time to get input from everyone on the team" shows that you've really been paying attention.

- **Praise should be immediate.** Whenever possible, show gratitude in the moment. Don't save your praise for a big talk—be generous with your generosity.

- **Praise should be personal.** If you can, talk about how the behavior you're highlighting made you feel, or how it made your life easier.

- **Praise should be public.** One-on-one praise is great but praising in public is even better. Take the opportunity to make the person you're praising feel famous by shining a spotlight on them.

- **Praise should be purposeful.** Try to connect your positive feedback to the big picture. Talk about how the behavior you saw was part of achieving a bigger goal. Connecting to a sense of purpose is incredibly powerful for people—take the opportunity of praise to remind them *why* their hard work is so important.

Leading with gratitude has enormous benefits that go beyond employee engagement. If you cultivate an attitude of appreciation toward the people you lead, whether at work, in a classroom, or at home, you'll ultimately become less defensive, more open, and more flexible.[15]

The personal benefits of gratitude

Everyone needs to be appreciated. Everyone wants to feel seen. And when you remember this and make the effort to recognize and thank the people around you, you'll kick off a positive feedback cycle that will benefit you, too.

The simple act of saying "thank you" to someone will not only lift their mood, it will also make *you* feel better. Research has proven that expressing gratitude makes people happier and more optimistic. Gratitude has also been shown to strengthen relationships.[16]

But the benefits of gratitude go even deeper than that. Practicing gratitude can actually rewire your brain. In one study, people who wrote down three things they were grateful for 21 days in a row became more optimistic—for the next *six* months. Gratitude significantly improves mental health both for people who are generally stable and for people who are struggling. Gratitude can boost your willpower and make you more patient. If you practice gratitude regularly enough, you might even start to find it more rewarding to give money away than to get money for yourself.[17]

Gratitude can improve your physical health, too. Thinking about things you're grateful for can literally reduce your levels of stress hormones. It can even reduce physical pain.[18]

Even a little bit of gratitude practice has incredibly long-lasting effects. In another study, people who sat down one day and wrote thank-you letters to people they knew showed more gratitude-related activity in their brains *months later.*[19]

Convinced yet? There are many ways to begin adding more gratitude to your life. You can borrow an idea from one of the research studies I just mentioned and write thank-you letters to people you know or start a journal where you jot down a few things you're thankful for every day. You can challenge yourself to do a random act of kindness every day— or challenge yourself to avoid complaining one day a week. When you're checking out at the grocery store or performing another small transaction, you can make the effort to look the person helping you in the eye and give them a genuine smile.

Practicing gratitude could be as simple as remembering to say "thank you" the next time your partner, roommate, or kid takes out the trash or does the dishes. Try it. See how it makes you both feel. I guarantee it'll make your whole household happier.

Gratitude and making people feel famous

In July 2015, I was in Vienna covering the world premiere of *Mission: Impossible—Rogue Nation* at the world-famous opera house. There were thousands of fans in the streets, hoping to get a glimpse of the star: Tom Cruise.

Cruise is known for spending hours on the red carpet; I saw him answering every question from every reporter, and talking to hundreds of fans. He was completely present with every single person he talked to. When he got to me, I felt the full power of that famous smile. I could see his assistant hovering at his arm, telling him to move on to the next mini-interview, but he stayed with me until he'd answered all my questions. Everyone was there to see him, but he made *me* feel like the most important person on that red carpet.

There's a reason Cruise is one of the most famous people on the planet, and I believe that attitude is a big part of it. Yes, he's got talent. And yes, he can sometimes come off as a little *too* intense, as anyone who saw him jumping on Oprah's couch can confirm. But he's also one of the hardest working people in Hollywood, famously doing all his own stunts, and known for taking the time to interact with every single fan he meets.[20]

That's gratitude in action: Cruise knows that his fans are ultimately responsible for his success. So he leads with gratitude, by spending time with the people who put him where he is. For a moment, he turns the power of his spotlight onto the person he's talking to. He's the star, but he makes the fan feel famous.

The dangers of excessive external validation

Everyone has an innate psychological need to be seen and accepted for who they are. This need is present even in infancy, and it never goes away.[21] But for some people, a moment in the spotlight can provide a rush of adrenaline that can actually become addictive, driving them to take extreme actions to keep the attention on them. In some cases, this unhealthy desire for attention at any cost comes from early experiences of rejection, such as rejection by a parent.[22]

A true craving for fame can be incredibly damaging, not just because it's shallow, but because it's unlikely to ever be satisfied. You might go viral on Twitter or even get yourself onto a reality show, but building the star power of a Top Gun like Tom Cruise is rare. Even if you aren't trying to become a celebrity, you can damage yourself psychologically by trying too hard to get praise or attention from others.

Seeking to be popular in the sense of being liked is a healthy impulse. If you want people to like you, you'll focus on strengthening your relationships and being a likable person. But if you try to be popular in the sense of achieving some kind of higher status, you're more likely to end up anxious or depressed.[23]

Why? Building relationships is largely under your control—if you listen, approach other people with genuine curiosity, and practice the other skills in this book, you will connect with people. But status depends on many factors you can't control, including fleeting trends and the behavior of other people. Putting your psychological health in the hands of other people, relying on them to make you feel like you're good enough, is never healthy.

How to make people feel famous

When I talk about making people feel famous, I'm not talking about giving them a taste of the shallow kind of fame that's fleeting and ultimately unsatisfying. I'm talking about a deeper kind of appreciation, one that will build a sense of true connection. I'm talking about making people feel seen for who they truly are and appreciated for all that they give to the world. This kind of appreciation is more than just shining a spotlight on someone for a moment, or saying "thank you," although both of those things can be part of this deep, connected appreciation. But ultimately, making people feel famous is a process that starts with some of the skills we've already discussed in this book, including curiosity and careful listening, and continues with a creative outward expression of gratitude.

What follows are my top five tips for making people feel famous.

Document their details

If you know you're going to meet someone who could be important to your life or career—a potential client or investor, someone interviewing you for a job, or a new partner's family—take a little time before the meeting and do your homework on them. Check out their social media feeds, read any articles they've written, and, especially for a professional meeting, take a few notes about top topics to bring up. Doing this work ahead of time will help you spark some genuine curiosity about them, and that interest will come through when you meet.

After meeting a new person, make some notes about the details they shared. We can only remember so much. If you've established some common ground in an initial conversation, like a shared interest, make some notes so you can come back to that topic and keep building that connection the next time you talk. Keep the notes somewhere you can refer to them before your next conversation. If you review your notes before you talk again, you'll give yourself the opportunity to surprise and delight your new friend by remembering the things they shared.

A few years back, I hosted the Canucks for Kids Fund Telethon. One of the head producers from Sportsnet was there, and as we chatted, we bonded over the fact that we had both adopted rescue dogs. He told me about this ESPN documentary on a dog called Arthur, who followed an adventure racing team over 6,000 miles as they hiked, mountain biked, and kayaked, until he was ultimately adopted by the leader of the team.[24] (It's an amazing story—just try to watch it without crying!)

Lori and I had recently adopted Smiley, a timid rescue dog from Thailand, through the Soi Dog Foundation. Lori had grown up with dogs, but I had been afraid of them ever since I got attacked by one when I was a kid. She convinced me to try living with a dog, and I'm so glad she did. Smiley was rescued from the dog meat trade. He was with us for five years until he got cancer, and we had to put him down. One of the worst days of our lives.

At the time I met this producer, though, Smiley was relatively new to our family. This guy lit up when he spoke about his own rescue dog, named Daisy. We talked and shared pictures and had a great conversation, and the telethon was a big success.

A year later, that same producer sent me an email, inviting me back to host the telethon again. I wrote back, thanked him, and agreed to come on board. I also asked, "How's Daisy?"

Within minutes, he picked up the phone and called me. "How the heck can you possibly remember my dog's name?" he asked.

When I ask questions and get personal answers, I make sure to document their details. After our conversation, I jotted down a few notes about who he was and what we'd talked about. It took me two minutes to do—and it cemented a genuine bond with someone I'd only met once. A year later, I was able to pick up that conversation where we'd left off and continue to build that relationship, all because I took two minutes out of my day to write down the word "Daisy."

A few minutes spent on notes the day you meet someone will go a long way toward building a genuine connection. It may feel artificial the first couple of times you do it but remind yourself that by taking the time to take notes, you are putting in the time and effort to foster a real connection. And that effort in itself is a form of caring.

Remember their name

A person's name is the most important word in any conversation. So why is it so hard to remember? Well, there are some good reasons.[25] Where most words always refer to the same thing—a rose is a rose is a rose—the name "Emily" can refer to any number of different people who happen to be named Emily. We don't say people's names that often, so they're not as easy to recall as more common words. And names don't have synonyms. If you forget the word "coffee" before you've had your coffee, you could say "java" or "cup of joe" or "the hot drink that comes in a mug, please give it to me, I need it." You could talk around your memory lapse. But if you forget Emily's name, there's no polite way to talk around that—you can't call her "blond lady" or "tall woman" and expect to continue having a nice chat.

Early in my career, I was a host on MTV Canada Monday to Friday. After a fun segment exploring what it takes to be a weathercaster with CTV News, I was offered a gig as the third-string weathercaster. I would basically be asked to fill in on the occasional weekend. I told the news director who offered me the job, "I've never done live television, and I don't know much about meteorology." His response: "Great, when can you start?"

He was a lot more confident about my ability to pick things up quickly than I was. The learning curve was pretty much vertical. When they needed me to fill in, I was both producing and presenting the weather. But it was a great opportunity for me to learn a lot of new skills, so I threw myself into it with everything I had.

During the holidays that year, the regular weather anchors both requested vacation time. I was asked to present with the main news anchor on a weeknight. He was a big deal, and this was a big moment for me. I was still trying to convince both Mom and Dad that this television thing wasn't just a hobby, but a viable career. The evening news was a big break.

The anchor came into the weather area an hour before the 6 o'clock news that day. He introduced himself and asked how to pronounce my name. The veteran came to the rookie, making me feel famous. I was on cloud nine. I felt respected, appreciated.

Once the broadcast was in full swing, I got into the weather position and watched the anchor read the headlines like a boss. The moment was coming where he would introduce me for my first weather hit. Mom and Dad, who were watching at home, could proudly tell their friends their son was on the news, and all would be good in the world.

The big moment came. He finished reading the first news segment. He said, "And now, for your first look at the holiday forecast, here's ... Raz Magoogey."

Raz Magoogey ... Move over, John Travolta.

Keep in mind, he's the veteran, I'm the rookie, and we're on live television. Those two words were a surprise that had me showcasing the "deer in headlights" look on my face—not how I wanted to start off my first live weather hit together. I awkwardly said "Thanks" and then began gesturing at the weather map, trying to remember what I was supposed to say. Something about an area of low pressure?

Sure, it was embarrassing then. Now, years later, I have a jacket that says "Raz Magoogey" on the back, thanks to a friend who knows we can laugh about it now that so much time has passed. But at the time, I definitely did not feel like laughing.

Despite the fact that forgetting names is a common experience, when someone forgets *our* name, we take it personally. (Especially if it happens on live television. With our parents watching.) Luckily, there are some good strategies out there that can help. One of my favorites is courtesy of Benjamin Levy, author of *Remember Every Name Every Time*. His approach is known as the FACE method—Focus, Ask, Comment, and Employ:[26]

1   When a new person is introducing themselves, **focus** your attention on their face to cement the connection between face and name.

2   **Ask** a question about their name—how it's spelled, or whether they prefer "Catherine" or "Cathy." That gives you another moment to focus on the name and hear it repeated once or twice.

3   **Comment** on the name: "My brother's name is Zain!" Now you're not only repeating the name, you're making a connection in your head that should help you remember it.

4   **Employ** the name again: "Nice to meet you, Rick." Repetition is your friend here.

I like this method, and I personally use a variation on it. Again, repetition is the key. Whenever I meet a new person, my goal is to "three-peat" their name to make sure it sticks. When they introduce themselves, I'll say the name out loud: "Nice to meet you, Linda." In the course of conversation, I'll ask a question using their name: "Linda, how did you meet our host?" And as we're wrapping up the conversation, I'll

Making people feel famous starts with curiosity and careful listening, and continues **with a creative expression of gratitude**.

thank them and use their name a third time: "Linda, thanks so much for walking me through that process."

Give them access

People value money, of course. They value career growth. But when it comes to connection, the thing they value most is *access*. Access to ideas, to people, to experiences. Particularly today, when the internet puts all the information in the world right at our fingertips, people are willing to pay a premium to get access to insider experiences or more intimate connections with leaders and celebrities.

Social media revolutionized the way we connect with the people we admire. It gave us all a backstage pass to our favorite stars. Getting a follow or retweet from your favorite star became a new kind of status symbol. Selfies became the new autographs. Reality shows like *American Idol*, *The Voice*, and *America's Got Talent* have given ordinary people a chance to become stars themselves on a mainstream platform. People love to show off when they meet someone famous or get that behind-the-scenes VIP moment.

One music teacher in Ontario got some amazing VIP treatment after she organized a creative activity for her students during quarantine. The teacher, Julia Jung, had been working hard to keep her students engaged while school was closed, including driving around and delivering school instruments to all the students so they could keep making music at home. One of her lockdown activities was getting her students to record a socially distanced cover of the song "Years in the Making" by the band Arkells. She reached out to the lead singer, Max Kerman, to tell him about the project. He got excited and talked to the students about it.

As if that weren't enough, Kerman, a massive Toronto Raptors fan who had previously invited head coach Nick

Nurse, a musician himself, to join him on stage in 2019 after the team won the NBA championship, reached out once again to do something special. Nurse had just launched a new foundation focused on education and mentorship. Nurse and Kerman put together a Zoom call to surprise Jung with the news that Nurse's foundation was donating $25,000 to her school so she could buy new instruments for her students.[27]

Talk about the VIP treatment! Especially at a moment when teachers were working so hard to stay connected with their students despite schools being closed, this was a beautiful gesture that must have made Jung feel incredibly special. And of course, Nurse's generous donation gave Jung's students a VIP moment of their own.

How can you create VIP moments for the people in your life? If you're a leader, pull back the curtain in your company and let your workers in on how things really work. With friends or even a new partner, go first and give access to personal secrets that will help you build trust and make others feel valued.

Show unsolicited appreciation

Christmases. Birthdays. Anniversaries. Retirements. Big events like these often bring thoughtful messages of gratitude sharing what we mean to people. Those messages are welcome at any time, of course—but what if we showed more appreciation when it was unexpected?

How? Remember to make your praise specific—call out a particular action and share how that action impacted you or the team. And try to tailor the moment of recognition to surprise and delight the person you're praising specifically. That could mean calling them out in a staff meeting, sharing a note of praise and cc'ing the big boss, or taking them out for a celebratory lunch. Maybe you could start a wall of fame in your office, or get the person a gift card related to a hobby they're involved in.

You can also use these general principles to appreciate people in other contexts. For example, if you want to show appreciation for a big client, get creative about the gift or treat you send, and write a note that goes beyond a generic thank you: "The whole team loved meeting all those inspirational kids at your fundraiser! Your project really brightened up our month!"

Think outside the box a little, even for milestone events: if you always send flowers for Mother's Day, why not mix it up and share a book about a strong woman who reminds you of your mom? According to John Ruhlin, the author of the book *Giftology*, the best gifts are personal, unique, and connected to the recipient's interests.[28] The meaning of a gift has nothing to do with its price tag—in fact, an expensive gift can come across as lazy if it's not tailored to the recipient. But a well-chosen, thoughtful, personal gift can create a powerful moment of connection.

Whenever possible, your moments of appreciation should connect back to a sense of larger purpose. A personal moment that stands out for me was an interview with Jenny Konkin, the president and cofounder of Whole Way House, a single-room occupancy on Vancouver's Downtown Eastside, along with Kris, a Whole Way House resident. Kris, like many people who've been supported by this amazing organization, has turned his life around through the power of human connection with his fellow residents in the house.

I will always remember the three simple words they shared with me: "I Get To."[29] Those three words rewired my brain. Instead of saying "What do I need to do to today?" or "What do I have to do?" I try to remember to ask myself, "What do I *get* to do today?" I *get* to work on a challenging new project. I *get* to spend time with my son. I *get* to change this dirty diaper. Trust me, it helps. When you move from a spirit of obligation to a spirit of gratitude, you will naturally be moved to share your appreciation with the people around you.

Create milestone moments

In their book *The Power of Moments: Why Certain Experiences Have Extraordinary Impact*, Chip Heath and Dan Heath explain that the defining moments that shape our lives share one or more of these four elements:[30]

1 **Elevation.** High-impact moments create a sense of elevated importance by appealing to the senses, raising the stakes, or flipping the script on what's expected.

2 **Insight.** Defining moments tell us something important that we didn't already know.

3 **Pride.** The moments we remember often make us feel proud of ourselves or someone we care about.

4 **Connection.** Memorable moments create a sense of shared meaning and deepen the ties between people.

We can use these principles to create milestone moments for the people in our lives. Give someone an experience they'll never forget—they'll certainly never forget the person who made that experience possible.

During the coronavirus crisis, a retired farmer in Kansas sent an N95 mask to New York State Governor Andrew Cuomo, along with a letter asking him to give the mask to a health care worker fighting the virus. The farmer, Dennis Ruhnke, did something generous because he felt moved by the stories he was hearing about health care workers putting themselves on the line to serve others.

Kansas State University then reached out to Ruhnke and awarded him an honorary bachelor's degree for this moving act of kindness. Ruhnke had actually had to quit school just a couple of credits short of a degree after his father died. KSU created an incredible milestone moment for this generous, loving man by giving him a sense of pride in what he had done and sharing the insight that his long career in agriculture made him more than eligible for a degree.[31]

Another coronavirus milestone moment came from an IKEA near Frankfurt, Germany. When the chairman of a local mosque approached the store's manager asking if the community could use the store's parking lot to pray for the closing prayers of Eid al-Fitr, the end of Ramadan, the manager immediately agreed.[32] This unusual milestone moment certainly flipped the script on what Eid prayers would normally look and feel like, and it also gave the community a sense of connection in a moment when the virus was enforcing so much isolation.

What milestone moments can you create for the people around you?

The habit of making people feel famous goes hand in hand with some of the other qualities we've already discussed in this book. If you appreciate the talents of the people around you, you're more likely to listen to what they have to say, be curious about their lives and perspectives, and offer them empathy when they're struggling. A spirit of generous gratitude could completely transform the way you interact with the people in your life, if you let it.

PART THREE

THE FUTURE OF HUMAN CONNECTION

CONNECT IN A VIRTUAL WORLD

Send an email and
then toss a coin—
those are **your odds
of being understood**.

I MAGINE YOU got a text or email from your boss that said: "Hey, can you get me the proposal by the end of the week?" Now imagine you wrote back: "OK."

What you meant to say was, "Sounds good to me, no problem." But your boss might easily read that response as: "Really? You think I don't have enough to do already? Fine. I'll get it done. I'll work overtime YET AGAIN to meet your CRAZY DEADLINES."

OK... that is a little dramatic. But it's true that even a seemingly simple response—two letters, in the case of "OK" can easily be misinterpreted. In fact, it's often the simplest messages that are *most* easily misunderstood in text-based communication.

Think about it: how do you feel when you get an "OK" text? Doesn't it come across as irritated? Maybe a little passive-aggressive?

Experts say that variations on "OK" in particular tend to be received as negative or even aggressive, even though "OK" is a perfectly common, acceptable thing to say in face-to-face conversation. According to internet linguist Gretchen McCulloch, short responses in text-based communications tend to sound terse, curt, or even rude.[1]

To make things even more complicated, generational differences and power dynamics can change the way we read certain types of text-based messages. Younger people tend to perceive more subtle differences in tone when they're reading emails and texts, while older people tend not to realize that there's a world of difference between "OK!" and "OK." People with more power, like a manager or supervisor in a workplace setting, also tend to spend less time thinking about nuances of tone. Why should your boss worry if that "OK" sounds curt? You've got to finish the project anyway. At the same time, you're likely to spend way more time worrying about a terse message from your boss than one from the guy in the next cubicle. After all, if your boss is annoyed with you, there could be serious consequences.

These kinds of miscommunications can, of course, happen in personal messages, too. If you have to bail on happy hour because you need to work late, and your friend responds to your sorry-can't-make-it text with an "OK," what's your gut reaction? Do you assume they're really busy at work too, and don't have time to write a longer message—or do you jump to the conclusion that they're offended, and you've got damage control to do?

Personal relationships can also come with power dynamics that may be less formal, but no less real, than those at work. Even as adults, sometimes our inner insecure teenager comes out and tells us that a certain friend or acquaintance is way cooler or more popular than we are. Our anxiety about fitting in will color the way we read texts from those people. And if you're dating someone you secretly believe is out of your league—forget it. An "OK" from a new romantic partner could ruin your whole day.

With all these complex dynamics swirling around, it's no wonder that fully 50% of texts and emails are misunderstood. Send an email and then toss a coin—those are your odds of being understood. And yet, we tend to assume that other people understand *our* texts and emails 90% of the time.[2] When you think about those odds, it's a wonder we can communicate over email or text at all.

Maybe we should switch to semaphore.

The problem with digital communication

Why is it so easy to misunderstand text-based communication? There are a few factors at work here. First and most obviously, in a text or email, all the nonverbal cues we normally rely on to understand someone's tone and intent are stripped away. There are probably 100 different ways you could say "OK" and communicate 100 different meanings, if you were talking to someone face-to-face. But when all you have to go on are those two letters—no facial expressions, no tone of voice, no body language—the message becomes ambiguous. And because of the way our brains are hard-wired to look for danger, when the meaning of a message is ambiguous, we often assume the worst.[3]

The stripped-down, unsatisfying, ambiguous nature of text-based communication is one reason why, when the coronavirus pandemic forced many of us to isolate ourselves in our homes, we instinctively turned to video-call platforms like Zoom. Pre-pandemic, in December of 2019, Zoom had about 10 million daily users. In April 2020, the platform was logging more than 300 million daily users.[4] If you couldn't have your staff meeting in your office, or visit your family, you could at least have those conversations *virtually* face-to-face.

But almost as soon as Zoom use spiked, so did conversations about Zoom fatigue. Introverts grumbled about extroverts scheduling too many Zoom happy hours. Remote workers fretted about how their colleagues might judge them for the appearance of their workspaces or the behavior of their kids.[5] Lagging connections sometimes made it impossible to tell if the meeting was totally appalled by your comment—or just frozen.

Why are video calls so tiring and unsatisfying? If you can see a person's face and hear their voice, shouldn't that solve all the problems involved in text-based communication?

"Not exactly," says Nick Morgan, the author of *Can You Hear Me? How to Connect with People in a Virtual World*. "Video is more insidious, because we think we're getting all the cues that we would get face-to-face," Morgan says.[6] On a video call, our three-dimensional faces are squashed into two dimensions. "It's as if your emotions were muted," Morgan says.

When we're talking to someone face-to-face, we're taking in an enormous amount of information from the way they're holding their body and their minute changes in facial expression, Morgan explains. But we're processing all that information unconsciously. That's part of why Zoom fatigue is so real—on a conscious level, we assume that because we can see and hear the other person, it's basically the same as an in-person conversation. But it's not. We're missing a lot of the richness of those nonverbal cues, and, as a result, we find ourselves struggling to connect.

The nature of the technology itself can create a kind of disconnect. Even tiny glitches in a connection that are barely noticeable on a conscious level can seriously disrupt that unconscious processing of facial expressions that we rely on so heavily in face-to-face talks. The slight lags in connection and the flattened nature of the information we're receiving over video calls also interrupt our ability to echo and mimic the facial expressions of the people we're talking to. In face-to-face conversation, we do this all the time, unconsciously of course, as another way to ensure we understand how the other person is feeling. It's a crucial part of building connection in conversation, and video calls undermine it, leaving us feeling disconnected.

Even if your connection is completely perfect, the format of the call undermines our ability to trust one another. Most people on video calls are looking at their screens to see the people they're talking to. It's natural—but on the other end of the call, anyone who's not looking directly at the camera looks like they're avoiding eye contact. We unconsciously read that as a signal that they're either bored by the conversation, or they're hiding something.

What's worse, most people on video calls are actually looking at their *own* faces most of the time.[7] Admit it—you do this. It's hard to look away. Because you can see yourself, you feel self-conscious. You feel like you're performing, rather than making an authentic connection.

In the end, video calls create a kind of cognitive dissonance. We see the other person, but we don't feel like they're really there. As the management professor Gianpiero Petriglieri has put it, "It's easier being in each other's presence, or in each other's absence, than in the constant presence of each other's absence."[8]

The risks of remote work

The coronavirus pandemic forced many of us to work from home—often for the first time. The transition was sudden and dramatic for many people. In the course of a day, you may have changed from commuting to an office to attempting to work from home, either alone and isolated, or in a home suddenly crowded with two working parents and kids who were supposed to be attending school on Zoom. The learning curve was steep.

In the midst of the crisis, the question on millions of people's minds was: "When can we go back to normal?" But there's increasing evidence that the new normal isn't going to look much like the pre-pandemic normal we remember. According to an April 2020 survey of CFOs by Gartner, 74% of companies plan to have at least a small number of their employees work from home permanently, and almost 25% plan to have as many as one in five employees permanently shift to remote work. And a survey of workers by Cushman & Wakefield found that 73% of employees are hoping that their companies will keep the work-from-home option on the table even after the pandemic is over.[9]

But even if some people are excited about potentially seeing more flexible remote work policies continue, for many people, working from home comes with real risks. For starters, the sudden switch to working from home has been disorienting for most people: in another survey, 85% of people said they needed more help from their employers to adjust to remote work.[10] And on a deeper level, surveys of several large companies found that a majority of people were feeling more lonely and more anxious since starting to work remotely.

Working from home can be a real challenge. Particularly for people who live alone, the isolation of being cut off from the office takes a real toll. But no matter what your family situation, therapists say that the removal of barriers between work life and home life can be challenging on its own.[11] Remote workers may struggle to establish the kinds of routines that help make life feel predictable and purposeful.

When presenting virtually, ask questions, take flash polls, and generate feedback frequently. **Make your audience feel heard**.

———————

Blurring the lines between work and home can make the days seem to blend into one another, with the weekend essentially the same as the weekdays. If you sleep, eat dinner, or play with your kids in the same place you work, you may start to feel like you're always at the office.

Remote workers can even feel pressured to work *more* than they would if they were in the office, in order to prove that they're remaining productive at home. Combined with the lack of routine and the removal of physical and mental barriers between work and home, that's a clear recipe for burnout. No wonder one pre-pandemic survey of remote workers in tech found that 82% felt burnt out.[12]

Long term, will companies stick with their plans to shift to more remote work? It's still too soon to know. But several tech giants have announced new policies,[13] and the trend isn't confined to Silicon Valley, either. Big, relatively conservative companies in the financial sector, including Barclays and Morgan Stanley, are also talking about using much less physical office space in the post-pandemic future.[14]

Certainly, remote work under the threat of a pandemic is uniquely stressful. And the inability to go out and socialize with friends and family after working hours pretty much destroys work-life balance. But many of the problems with remote work are problems regardless of what's going on in the world outside your home office. Virtual communication, even video calls, is unsatisfying and stressful. Miscommunication is incredibly common in emails, texts, and Slack channels. And, on a very basic level, if you don't go into the office, you miss out on the shared experiences office life creates: the small talk about the weather or the traffic, the chance meetings in the kitchen, the opportunity to stop by a colleague's desk for a quick chat when you get up to stretch your legs or refresh your coffee.

So, if many of us are going to be working remotely at least part of the time for the long haul, what do we do about it? How can we make our virtual communication better, richer, and more satisfying?

Best practices for virtual communication

When you learn that 50% of texts and emails are misunderstood, what's your gut reaction? Do you think, "Surely not *my* emails. I am always 100% clear"? Or, "People are idiots. How could anyone misunderstand my emails?"

That's the wrong question to ask, according to Nick Morgan. "The right question is, 'how can I make my intent clear?'" The key is to remember that, as humans, on a gut level we care more about the *intent* behind someone's words than the words themselves. When we're reading an email or sitting down for a Zoom meeting, the first and most important thing we want to know is, can I trust this person? Are they on my side? Are they being open and honest with me? "Intent is what we humans care about more than anything else," Morgan says, "We get virtually all the real information about that unconsciously, from your attitude."

Because those unconscious, nonverbal signals are stripped out from virtual communication, when you are communicating remotely you need to focus on communicating your intent. Here are some best practices for communicating intent in a virtual space.

Use emojis in text-based messages
Depending on your age and the industry you work in, you may think of emojis as unprofessional or frivolous. "Get over it," Morgan says. "Start using them." A simple smiley

face can completely change the way a message is received. Which email would you rather receive: "got it" or "got it ☺"? If you're not fluent in emoji, keep it simple. Stick to basic icons like smiley faces and thumbs-ups. It doesn't take much to change the perceived tone of a message.

Use more emotional words in voice or video calls

One simple way to convey your intent is to use words to describe it. Instead of saying "Happy to be here" when you're introduced in a meeting, try saying something like, "I'm excited to talk to you all!" or "I'm thrilled to be starting this conversation." If the conversation is going in a direction that concerns you, name your concern: "I'm worried we're forgetting about the customer experience." Remember, your emotions will be flattened by the technology you're using. Using some emotional words will help people "read" your intent and contextualize your suggestions.

Amp up your energy

If you say you're thrilled with a flat voice and motionless face, you'll come across as insincere. But if you lean forward, speak with some gusto, and focus on believing what you're saying, you'll start to communicate the way you intend to. "What we really need," says Morgan, "is people who are empathetic and who amp up the emotion without obsessing too much about what's happening on your face or in your body language." In other words, it's better to focus on *feeling* excited rather than plastering on a big smile.

Hide your self-view on video calls

As you probably know from experience, it's almost impossible to look away from your own face when it's in view. But being able to see your own face makes you self-conscious—and if you really want to clearly communicate your intent, you need to be focusing on the person you're talking to. Hide that self-view and keep your focus where it belongs.

Practice a little

Here's a little trick Morgan uses when coaching clients: the happy-sad game. Record yourself reading the same short speech once as if you're really happy, and once as if you're terribly sad. Then watch the playback. You'll probably find that what felt like a big, obvious emotion to you in the moment doesn't come through in video. "Learn to calibrate what shows up, because it is a performance," Morgan says. "And you need to learn what works for you individually."

Make it interactive

Partly because emotion is muted over video calls—and partly because all the temptations and distractions of the internet are right there—it can be very hard for people to stay focused on a long Zoom call. When presenting virtually or hosting a remote meeting, ask questions, take flash polls, and generate feedback frequently. Make your audience feel heard. "People want to be seen, and they want to feel like their voice matters in this conversation," Morgan says.

The most important thing you can do to make your intent come through in virtual communication is to recognize how limited these technologies really are. If you know that half of all texts or emails are misunderstood, if you know that emotion is muted even on video calls, where it feels like you can see the person and read their facial expressions—if you know all this, you're already on your way to correcting the problem. Simply knowing that you need to work harder to communicate intent in virtual communication will start you down the path to communicating more clearly.

If you feel inauthentic or awkward trying to use more emojis, more emotional language, and more energy in your virtual communication, don't despair. Practice really does lead to progress. With practice, all these techniques will begin to feel more comfortable. You'll find your own style of virtual communication that feels authentic to you and gets your intent and emotion across.

We all became broadcasters

Life in isolation led to one of the most fascinating social experiments of our lifetime. The sudden transition to a work-from-home, socially distanced world created an unexpected universal experience: we all became live broadcasters.

From personal experience I can share that hosting a live television show where you present information and interview guests poses a unique set of challenges. You need to be uber-focused at all times. You have to listen intently and roll with the punches when things go sideways.

And that's when everyone is in the same room. Throw in a videoconference dynamic, what we in the business would call "satellite junkets," and all bets are off.

In a satellite interview, you're lucky if you get 60 seconds during a commercial break to chat with the guest to warm them up before the interview begins. You're looking right into the camera, so you can't see or read your guest's body language. You have to rely on their voice. Sometimes there are up to five-second time delays. Oh, and the signal can drop at any time.

Sound familiar?

I've had plenty of fun moments during these satellite interviews. Hugh Jackman once told me that he still sits in theaters incognito to watch his movies on opening weekend to see how the audience reacts. He also shared that he wears the Wolverine costume in the bedroom to spice things up. Talk about commitment to your craft.

Michael Caine shared that the secret to 40 years of marriage was separate bathrooms. This is a commandment I live by every day.

But when I participated in one of my first *live* satellite interviews on *Breakfast Television Vancouver*, that was a conversation I'll never forget.

When the Los Angeles Kings were up 2–1 in the 2010 NHL Western Conference Quarter-Finals against the Vancouver Canucks, our *Breakfast Television* team decided to reach out to the *KTLA 5 Morning News* to have some fun and make a friendly wager. Their producers obliged but made a point of saying their anchors wouldn't wear a Canucks jersey if things went our way. That said, they were open to a fun conversation on the air.

When we went live into KTLA's morning show from Vancouver, I couldn't see any of their anchors, I could only hear them in my earpiece. On television, it looked like a Zoom chat with fancy graphic animations. They had two news anchors in their main studio and a sports anchor, Roger Lodge, the former host of the hit show *Blind Date*, in a different one.

When they asked what the stakes for the bet were, I said if the Canucks came back and won (remember, we were down 2–1 in the series), Roger would have to wear a Canucks jersey on their show and send me an autographed *Blind Date* host headshot. Apparently, he didn't appreciate the reminder of his reality show past.

Well, Roger said that was a "wimp bet." He upped the ante and said if the Kings beat the Canucks, I'd have to appear

Nobody is expecting
perfection in the
virtual format, but your
audience will appreciate
you **owning the
unscripted moments**.

---

on my show in nothing but a Speedo. And if the Canucks beat the Kings, he would do his show in nothing but a Speedo.

This was one of my first live satellite chats. You could see the blood rush out of my face. I was mortified. A friendly bet just got ugly. These chicken legs in a Speedo on LIVE television? My so-called career would be over.

Turns out the Canucks won the next three games. The Canucks clinched the series with a Game 6 win on a Sunday night. I watched the game at home with Dad. He smiled and said, "I guess you don't have to wear a Speedo to work tomorrow morning." I think he was even more relieved than I was.

Roger attempted to back out of the bet that Monday morning. With the help of a Facebook Fan Page, "Speedogate," not to mention the Metro Vancouver newspaper backing our cause with a front-page article calling him out, he finally surrendered and wore the red thong I had sent him two days later live on the air. This time, I had a monitor to react. You can't unsee things like this. I've never met Roger in person, but I can tell you that *that* conversation counted!

What started as a friendly virtual exchange intensified into a little bit of chaos, live on air. But we both rolled with it and in the end, everybody won.

Well, maybe not everybody.

Virtual communication can be unpredictable, but there are many ways to approach it to make your presence memorable. Speedos are just one option. Nobody is expecting perfection in the virtual format, but your audience will appreciate you owning the unscripted moments, whether you're giving a presentation, leading a meeting, or simply trying to connect.

How to engage an audience when you're not in the same room

Even after the fear of the coronavirus pandemic has faded, remote meetings are likely to be part of our lives. The cost savings and convenience of meeting in virtual space instead of getting on a plane or even a subway car to meet face-to-face are just too compelling—even though we all feel the limitations of these virtual meetings on a gut level.

So how can you make your virtual meetings feel intimate and interactive? Here are my top 10 tips for enhancing your presence in a virtual meeting or presentation.

Engage them early

Your meeting or presentation actually starts hours, if not days, before the scheduled time. Well before a presentation, you should figure out what your audience's top priorities are, so you can structure your content to be meaningful to them. If you're presenting at a conference, talk to the organizers and eavesdrop on some social media conversations among your likely audience. If you're presenting in a meeting, you should know what's top of mind for the team—use that information to stay laser-focused on what matters most.

When the meeting is set to begin, sign in to the video call about five minutes early so you can start connecting with people informally. Then start your actual talk with a quick check-in. People logging in to virtual events are often distracted or overwhelmed by life outside the frame of the camera. Try asking a simple question like, "In one word, how are you feeling?" Or ask people to drop a few lines in the chat box to share where they're coming from and what they're hoping to get out of the presentation.

Whenever possible, address people by name. Remember, a person's name is the most important word in any conversation.

Speak with your space

As soon as your camera is live, before you've said a word, your space is telling a story. Think about the popularity of social media accounts like Bookcase Credibility (@BCredibility) and Room Rater (@ratemyskyperoom). In a virtual meeting, viewers are getting a glimpse of your life behind the scenes.

We are all curious creatures, with an insatiable appetite for information. Over Zoom, people are looking at your bookshelf, your artwork, the photos on your wall. They want to know more about you. They're also making assessments of who you are, how you live, and what you're about before you've said a word.

What story do you want your space to tell, and how can you share more information in the frame? If you know you're talking to a group of parents, maybe you want to show some toys or your children's artwork in the background to make yourself relatable. If you're in a business meeting, have your place clean and organized to showcase professionalism. Whatever the occasion, make your space interesting, but not distracting.

Use good lighting and get a professional microphone to make a strong impression. Test your tech before the meeting, so you're not fumbling through things when your audience is watching.

Avoid using virtual backgrounds. The two-dimensional screen experience is already blocking the normal social cues of seeing someone breathe, nod their head, move their eyes. Bring your audience into a real space, so they can authentically connect with you as a person instead of struggling to relate to you and a potentially alienating background.

Hook them with a story

There are a number of effective ways to start a presentation. You can ask a question, share a shocking statistic, or dive right in with a provocative statement. But in the virtual environment, I believe story is the most effective way to engage an audience.

When you start with a story, you make your audience feel something real right away. You hook them with an emotional roller coaster. The more authentic you can be, the more you'll connect with your audience. Think about the questions the people in your audience are asking themselves and choose a story that speaks to those concerns. Build your narrative around their priorities, not yours.

Interact with your scene

To be more interesting on camera, bring life and real presence into your presentation. How? Interact with your scene. Be the three-dimensional person you would be in a face-to-face meeting.

Use props. Have a coffee mug or something on hand that shows some personality. For me, it's a Toronto Raptors "We the North" hat. Let people see you pick up a pen and write things down. Have a flip chart beside you to capture ideas. These are natural actions that you'd see in a face-to-face meeting. You want to interact with your environment in a way that feels more real and adds visual appeal for your audience.

Look at the camera, not your audience

This one is almost counterintuitive. It's easy to get distracted by looking at people in those boxes on the screen. You want to feel connected to the people you're speaking to. But unfortunately, looking at those faces will "read" to your audience as you *avoiding* eye contact.

You've got to learn the broadcaster's trick of looking at the camera but pretending you're speaking to a room full of people. Remember to amplify your energy, your gestures, and your emotion so your audience can feel your words through the lens.

When you make your point, pause. Let them digest it. Forget about the immediate sensory feedback you're probably used to. You will not get it virtually. You might get some comments in the chat box, but expect and embrace the silence you will hear, as it's normal in this format.

Focusing on the camera with your eye contact is such an important point to create a sense of intimacy. If you're presenting using notes, go with bullet points and keep your current talking point at the top of your computer screen as close to the web camera as possible, so it feels like a conversation is happening versus you just reading notes out loud.

Watch the playback after the meeting. Talking on camera may be new for you. Ask for the playback link and analyze your eye contact and the energy you are putting out for the audience. This visual feedback will help you improve for your next event.

Become a broadcaster

We all became broadcasters when videoconferencing took over during coronavirus isolation. The key difference between our remote presence versus our in-person presence is how we describe what's happening.

For example, you may have heard of the traditional speaking formula "Tell them what you're going to tell them, tell them, then tell them what you told them." In the virtual space, giving the audience that play-by-play, drawing out the thought map, makes it easy for people to follow along.

When audience members ask questions, keep that play-by-play going. Recognize the questioner first. Make sure the entire audience knows who asked the question and where they're coming from. Then pause, reflect on the question, and answer it with enthusiasm and appreciation.

Throughout the presentation, describe what you're doing. Are you reading the chat box, are you taking notes? Are you looking up a specific piece of research on your screen? Bring the audience into your experience. It's easy to look distracted in the virtual medium. Describing your actions helps establish purpose and intent.

Switch up your speaking modes

Capturing your audience's attention is the first challenge. But keeping it is an even bigger challenge—especially when they're dialing in from home, where it's so easy to become distracted.

Your goal, whether you're running a meeting or giving a talk, is to achieve consistent engagement. Start by setting expectations: Why are you meeting today? Is the goal to share a status update, make a decision, solve a problem, strengthen relationships? Set an intention for the meeting that gives the audience something to do, so they have a reason to stay engaged.

Keep in mind that attention spans are much shorter in the virtual setting because of all the potential distractions. You're competing for your audience's attention with the emails coming in on their computers, the texts coming in on their phones, the siren call of their social media apps, and family members who may be making noise in the background or outright interrupting them. At the same time, as an image on a screen, you are much less engaging than you would be as a live human in the room. According to media theorist Douglas Rushkoff, the author of the book *Team Human*, when you're in a live audience, your eyes follow a speaker as they move across the stage or around the room.

But in a virtual meeting, you're locked into a fixed gaze, staring at the screen, where it's easy to lose focus and even fall into a kind of half-asleep state.

If you're scheduled to speak over a videoconference for more than 10 minutes, it's vital that you switch things up periodically. I recommend breaking to ask a question or otherwise engage the audience in doing something active about every 7 to 10 minutes. Take an audience poll; read some feedback in the chat; share people's thoughts. Then speak for another 7 to 10 minutes, and then switch it up again.

In the case of formal presentations, a Q&A is a really powerful way to make a speech feel like a conversation. Plan some questions with the host of the event that are real and create a sense of urgency as to what's happening right now. Then once you get rolling, start answering audience questions.

Over videoconference, it's particularly easy for people to fall into the bystander effect. This is a psychological phenomenon, more formally known as "diffusion of responsibility," in which people are less likely to take action when in the presence of a large group of strangers. So you're in your Zoom chat, and you throw out a question, and... crickets. People are waiting for someone else to jump in. If you are the speaker and have good relationships with some of your attendees, call on them by name to help avoid the dead air. You can also have a few backup questions to ask to trigger thoughts and ideas from your group to help bypass the bystander effect.

Some events lend themselves well to breakout rooms. This is a great way to get the audience engaged. Send them off with a task and a question for 5 or 10 minutes, then have them report back. One popular technique for adaptive learning is the "Think-Pair-Share" method: throw out a question, give them some time to think about it, then get your group to pair up in breakout rooms to share their thoughts. Then have them report back afterward in your main room. Reporting back gives the audience a chance to feel heard.

Engagement triggers like these are vital with virtual presentations. The more actively involved the audience is, the more they will listen and take action long after the presentation is over.

Consistency cultivates trust

If you're speaking, have your host introduce you not just with your formal bio, but with a story or experience that humanizes who you are and what makes your accomplishments unique. This can help move your audience emotionally and encourage them to connect with you before you've even said a word. As a host and MC, this has always worked well on stage, and I've found it is equally effective in the virtual setting.

Remember, it's harder to read people's nonverbal cues and understand their personalities through a screen. Consistency is key if you want to build trust with an audience, a client, or a group of colleagues you don't already know well. If you're the joker cracking one-liners in email, and then you present with a serious tone and deadpan delivery in a meeting, people will wonder who the real you actually is. Whatever your vibe is—humor, edge, warmth—keep it consistent to help cultivate trust.

Practice, record, repeat

Being on camera could be a whole new experience for you, and at first it can feel overwhelming. You might be thinking, "How do I look?" "Is that what I really sound like?" "Did I smile enough?"

When I first got into the television business almost 20 years ago, I asked a seasoned host and reporter, "How long did it take you to get comfortable being in front of the camera?"

In a medium where communication can be difficult, taking a few minutes to connect with real emotion before you get down to work **could make all the difference**.

He'd been in the business over 15 years. He said, "I'm still figuring it out."

That always stuck with me. Throughout my entire television career, I would watch the playback after every show and interview to review how I presented and how I could improve. I'd look at pace, posture, micro-expressions, fully recognizing that it all gets better with practice.

Record yourself on camera, review it, ask someone you trust for feedback, and repeat the process. Repetition will help you gain confidence in front of the camera and help you improve for your future virtual presentations.

Embrace unpredictability

For me, the thrill of doing live television over the years has been the rush of presenting something important while knowing full well that things could go sideways at any time. How do you get over the fear of something going wrong? Embrace the unpredictability and just be where you are.

Maybe your child runs in and wants your attention, or the cat makes a cameo and Zoom-bombs your presentation... or someone challenges you to wear a Speedo. Roll with the punches. Smile, laugh it off, and have fun with it.

When in doubt, laugh

Virtual communication can do a lot to keep us connected, as many of us discovered when the coronavirus pandemic forced us into isolation. We can text, email, FaceTime, Zoom... we can communicate across distances in a way that would have been unimaginable to previous generations.

But virtual communication, as we've seen in this chapter, has some real limitations. Video calls, as technologically amazing as they are, simply aren't the same as face-to-face conversations.

One crucial thing we lose when we're isolated from other people is laughter. We are 30 times as likely to laugh with another person as we are to laugh by ourselves.[15] Laughter is a key part of the social glue that holds us together. Neurologically, laughter releases dopamine, which not only makes us healthier and happier, it can even help us pay better attention, learn more, and be more productive.

So the next time you're scheduled to join a virtual meeting, take a minute before the call starts to get yourself in a joyful frame of mind. Get to a place where the smile on your face is going to be genuine. And don't rush too quickly into the business of the meeting—check in first. Share a funny story about your life. In a medium where communication can be difficult, taking a few minutes to connect with real emotion and even laughter before you get down to work could make all the difference.

THE FUTURE IS HUMAN

———

No matter what crises come to test us, human nature doesn't change. The urgent need to gather face-to-face, to feel connected, to build relationships—**those drives are part of what makes us human**.

THE 1918 FLU pandemic killed 50 million people. Many communities locked down to slow the spread of the virus. Without modern technology to enable communication, people were profoundly isolated. In some places, that isolation turned into fear and suspicion. "People were actually afraid to talk to one another," according to one survivor. Communal ties frayed; people stopped taking care of their neighbors.[1]

It would have been understandable if someone living through that pandemic had predicted that society would never be the same. How could people let go of the fear of contagion? How could communities rebuild trust in their leaders, and in one another? Maybe people would turn away from communal gatherings for a generation. Maybe society would be profoundly and permanently changed.

And yet, the 1918 pandemic was immediately followed by the Roaring Twenties: jazz, flappers, speakeasies, movies. People threw themselves into socializing and gathering in groups with renewed enthusiasm. The economy roared, too, with construction and manufacturing thriving and cars and electricity reaching the masses.[2]

No matter what crises come to test us, human nature doesn't change. The urgent need to gather face-to-face, to feel connected, to build relationships—those drives are part of what makes us human. No virus can change that.

10 years in 10 weeks

Human nature never changes. But human societies do. And pandemics tend to accelerate those changes. As the historian Yuval Noah Harari has said, emergencies tend to "fast-forward historical processes."[3] The Black Death in Europe eventually spelled the end of the feudal system.[4] Yellow fever forced French troops to withdraw from Haiti, helping to ensure the lasting success of the rebellion of enslaved persons there.[5] And it was Europeans' immunities to diseases like smallpox and measles that enabled them to survive first contact with the peoples of the Americas, while those diseases decimated the New World's established Indigenous societies.

Without pandemics, human history would have unfolded very differently. How will the coronavirus pandemic shape history? As Andrew Yang, the entrepreneur and former Democratic candidate for president of the United States, put it, "We're experiencing 10 years of change in 10 weeks."[6]

When the coronavirus pandemic hit, almost overnight, businesses around the world shifted to remote work, and teachers and students jumped into online learning. Suddenly, many of us were living in one version of a technology-enabled future: an all-virtual world. And we were experiencing all the limitations and challenges of that world.

It's impossible to say exactly how this pandemic will reshape our lives in the long term. But one thing I do know for certain is that the human desire for connection will never change. That's why I believe that the best question to ask right now is not "What will the world of work look like in 2030?" but "How do we create human connection no matter where we are and what limitations we're working with?"

Living through 2020 forced many of us into a complete reset of our habits. Desperation and the human drive to connect, no matter what, made us double down on reimagining how we could still connect with each other despite the need for social distancing. We had to reexamine how we could contribute to our communities.

The pandemic reinvented our relationships with one another and with technology. The culture of convenience had already showed us what was possible: working from anywhere, communicating virtually, and having food, fitness, and fun available on demand. Uncertainty and grief tested us, but the silver lining of life in isolation was the creativity with which we reached out and found new ways to connect. Together, we explored new uses for the technology we thought we knew so well.

So where will we go from here? Our desire to seek out the company of one another will never disappear. This generation's "Roaring Twenties" are coming. The future will be different—it has to be—but it will still be human. We will still crave each other's company, physical touch, the excitement of live events experienced with a crowd.

At work, I do believe many companies will shift to hybrid structures, with many more people working remotely long term. Leaders will need to prioritize people and relationships as they work through this shift. Sales teams will need to lead with listening and revisit their value proposition. The customer experience will need to become more efficient while maintaining a focus on human connection on the front line.

The possibilities for connection and exploration in the virtual world are endless. We'll see a continued flowering of creativity and innovation in the digital space. But the five habits of human connection that we've covered in this book will continue to be vital for building strong relationships that will thrive now and in the future—whatever shape it takes.

Five predictions for the future of human connection

The shape of history will be changed by this pandemic. But I believe it's possible to get a sense of what our future might look like by using enduring truths about the human desire for connection as our guide. In the rest of this chapter, I'll share five predictions for the future of human connection—and share how you can navigate those changes by keeping the urgent need for strong relationships in mind.

New choreography for connection

For many people, the coronavirus upended our usual greeting rituals. Handshakes and hugs were out. People scrambled to come up with substitutes—maybe we bump elbows? Many experts believe that even after the coronavirus is merely a memory, it will take some time for greetings involving touch to feel comfortable again.[7]

Losing these greeting rituals isn't just a cause of temporary social awkwardness. Physical touch releases oxytocin, an essential hormone that promotes bonding and closeness. Positive touch strengthens our immune systems, improves our sleep, and even helps regulate digestion.[8] Touch starvation is a serious form of deprivation, one that was made vividly real for the thousands of people who were living alone when the coronavirus lockdowns began.

Touch starvation increases stress and makes us more susceptible to anxiety and depression. We discussed in Part One how isolation can create a vicious cycle, in which loneliness makes us more likely to perceive threats in the world around us, and that perception of threat makes us withdraw from the world even more. Touch starvation is an important part of that cycle. It's the physical, hormonal part of loneliness, and it can be debilitating.

In the long term, stress and isolation can impact our concentration, our ability to focus, and our memory.[9] No wonder so many of us found it difficult to focus during the coronavirus pandemic, especially during those first disorienting, frightening months. Burnout, already a huge problem in our modern hyper-connected, always-on work culture, became even more likely as the boundaries between work and home eroded.

During the coronavirus crisis, many people found it particularly difficult to look away from the news, whether on television or on social media. I believe this phenomenon was part of that vicious cycle of isolation. Of course, when major news events break, it's natural to look for answers. And part of what made the pandemic so stressful was that the news about the virus was uncertain and in flux for months, as scientists raced to learn what they could about the disease and how to fight it. But isolation, with its tendency to prime us to look for threats in the world around us, probably reinforced that impulse to keep our eyes glued to our news feeds.

Boundaries are crucial when it comes to fighting stress and burnout. One way to fight that tendency to spiral into anxious thoughts is to set a limit on the amount of time you'll spend reading the news or otherwise focusing on the thing you're worrying about.

But another way to fight stress and burnout is simply to connect with another person.[10] During the lockdown phase of the coronavirus crisis, experts recommended setting up a "buddy check-in" system with a friend. You'd plan to connect with this person every day, using the acronym "HELP" to guide your chats: ask How they're doing; be Empathetic and understanding; Listen without judgment and share any concerns; and then Plan next steps. This kind of check-in is a great way to strengthen an existing relationship, and it can help prompt you to do some self-reflection, too.

In times of crisis, connection becomes even *more* important. Just as isolation increases stress, anxiety, and depression, connection fights it.

That's why I believe we will return to physical greetings pretty quickly, once the virus has passed. And I believe we'll appreciate those simple things, like a hug from a friend, all the more for having missed them during the pandemic.

In the meantime, there are plenty of different ways to greet people. Cultures around the world have different customs, many of which don't involve touch. Bowing, for example, is common in several countries, including Japan, India, Nepal, Thailand, Laos, and Cambodia. In Tibet, people often stick out their tongues in greeting. And in Malaysia, people put their hands on their hearts and nod, indicating their open hearts and goodwill.[11] If handshakes are on hiatus for a while, I'd love to see this beautifully symbolic gesture catch on.

Relationship-first leadership

During the height of the pandemic, the question on everyone's minds was, "How and when will we go back to work?" Corporate leaders were grappling with the question of how to safely reopen their offices; working parents were worrying about what they'd do if the office was open but school or day care wasn't. It's clear that even as the most urgent phase of the coronavirus crisis passes, the future will be complicated and patchwork. Many of our assumptions about what knowledge work looks like are going to be tested.

In the near future, for those of us who do return to working in an office, that office is likely to look different than it did pre-pandemic. Open-plan offices will have to be reconfigured so that workstations don't face each other and people can sit farther apart. Communal lounge areas and even conference

In times of crisis, connection becomes even *more* important. Just as isolation increases stress, anxiety, and depression, **connection fights it**.

rooms may disappear. Desks will have to be kept clear for regular deep cleaning.[12]

Some companies may respond by deciding not to return to large, centralized offices at all. On the flip side, some may take advantage of falling real estate prices and add *more* space so that they can create safer, socially distanced offices. These new offices could even be beautiful. Some architects are already starting to think about new pandemic safety features that, incidentally, sound pretty great: windows that open, wider hallways, roof gardens, even outdoor escalators and private terraces for every office.[13]

But for now, at least, most companies are expecting some kind of return to office life: a June 2020 survey by Xerox found that 82% of the workforce is expected to be back in the office within 12 to 18 months—in other words, by the second half of 2021. At the same time, 58% of companies said they planned to change their work-from-home policies, and substantial majorities of companies in several countries, including Canada, the United States, the United Kingdom, Germany, and France, said the pandemic experience had increased their confidence in remote work.[14]

I believe the future of office life is going to be a hybrid of office-based work and remote work. This pandemic experience was a huge test for organizations. Many found that their systems, particularly their systems for remote collaboration, weren't quite prepared for a 100% remote workforce. But companies have been investing in strengthening those systems during this crisis period, and by the time the coronavirus is fully in our rear-view mirror, remote-work technology will be battle-tested and ready.

The technology exists to make a hybrid work culture possible. And for many people, the idea is alluring. If you're not trying to work from home while also homeschooling your kids during an incredibly stressful global pandemic, remote work does have its perks. For some people, there's a real appeal to the idea that you could choose to go into an office on certain days—for meetings with colleagues, for example—and choose to work remotely on others—say, when you need to do deep, focused work without any interruptions. (Schools would be open in this scenario.) You could even choose to work from a vacation house for a couple of weeks, or work from a friend's or family member's house to enable a longer visit. Don't think of it as work from home—call it work from anywhere.[15]

As nice as the idea of working from a beach house sounds, there are plenty of challenges ahead if we do move to a truly hybrid work model. During the coronavirus pandemic, 65% of employers said it had been tough to maintain employee morale, and more than a third of companies reported problems with company culture.[16]

Of course, morale was never going to be sky-high during such a stressful event as a global pandemic. But maintaining a cohesive, positive corporate culture with a substantial number of employees working from home will be difficult under any circumstances. When they're not in the office, people miss out on the spontaneous, casual conversations they might have in hallways or in the kitchen. It's harder to create a sense of community when you only see your colleagues for Zoom meetings.

I believe the key to thriving in the hybrid workforce of the future will be *relationship-first leadership*. When people are working remotely, connection and community don't happen organically in the same ways they do when the whole team is in the office. You can't rely on the break room, the after-work happy hour, or free bagels on Tuesdays to do the work of team-building for you. You have to be intentional about building strong relationships under these conditions.

That means drawing on the five habits of human connection that we've been discussing throughout this book. Leaders should begin with listening. They should cultivate authentic curiosity about the people they work with. They should show some vulnerability to help people feel comfortable being vulnerable and imperfect themselves. They should be assertively empathetic, welcoming different viewpoints and managing conflict through listening and striving to understand. And they should make people feel famous, going out of their way to show appreciation as often as they can.

Relationship-first leadership means focusing on connection first, productivity second. I believe the research on employee engagement proves that happy, connected people work harder, anyway. Creating a supportive, connected corporate culture is the best way to keep people motivated and create an atmosphere that supports creativity. It's also the best way to combat the isolation that can too easily creep in when people work from home.

Service before sales

The coronavirus pandemic immediately upended the world of sales. The *New York Times* profiled one salesperson, Josh Harcus, at SoftBank Robotics America, whose pre-COVID life involved extensive travel to demo $6,000 robotic vacuums to corporate clients. When the lockdowns began, Harcus started doing Zoom demos to potential clients—and found that his sales were still strong. Suddenly, spending hours flying across the country just to do a 10-minute demo the way he used to seemed crazy.[17]

Whether or not one robot vacuum salesperson goes back to in-person demos, it's clear that the world of selling has changed. The *New York Times* profile noted that Harcus changed the way he spoke to clients as well as switching to

Zoom: he started talking more about child care woes, knowing that many of his clients were struggling with the same lockdown issues he was. I believe that kind of empathy is going to be the key to sales success in the future.

The coronavirus crisis challenged our assumptions and priorities, both individually and socially. Many of us realized that we spent a lot of time and money pre-pandemic on things that we really didn't need. Being separated from friends and family has reminded us how much our relationships matter. And collectively, we've recognized what kinds of work are essential to the economy and to everyone's safety. We've also seen the Black Lives Matter movement re-emerge into popular consciousness with renewed urgency. These experiences will shape our new normal after the pandemic threat has passed.

To succeed in this new world, salespeople will have to learn how to meet customers where they are and understand their new priorities. They will have to lead with listening and empathy.

That starts with researching and understanding their new pain points. Don't assume you know where your customers are coming from now. Dive back into customer research. Reach out and listen to understand where they're at now and what they need most. Draw on all the skills we discussed in the "Listen without Distraction" chapter to make sure you're really listening with no preconceptions.

Next, reevaluate your value proposition. Maybe the thing that set you apart from competitors isn't as relevant now as it used to be.[18] Maybe your customers are more price conscious than they used to be, or maybe they're prioritizing great tech support because they're continuing to work remotely. If you've done your research, you should know what your customers' new priorities are and how you fit in.

But the listening doesn't stop with customer research. If you're doing person-to-person selling, you need to lead with listening during those meetings. Even after the immediate crisis has passed, I recommend not jumping back into "business as usual" mode. Start every meeting by acknowledging the situation. Make sure you know who you're talking to—are they grieving? Has their organization been through layoffs? Then move forward in a collaborative spirit. Let them tell you what they need, and then share how you believe you can help meet those needs.

A customized, personalized approach will be even more crucial going forward. Make customers feel heard and valued by showing them you respect the constraints they're working under. Work with them on pricing as much as you can and customize support solutions to meet their needs.

A reinvented customer experience

The customer experience of the future is going to have to be all about human connection—supported by automated systems for efficiency. I spoke to Curtis Christopherson, the president and CEO of Innovative Fitness, about how his company is reinventing the customer experience for a post-pandemic world. He believes the future of fitness is flexibility.

During the pandemic, Innovative Fitness, like many other fitness companies, shifted quickly to an all-remote, at-home workout model. "Our clients received 95% of the traditional experience, with 100% of the convenience of training at home," Christopherson says. Training through a screen created an equal obligation for both trainer and client to keep focused on each other for the entire hour. Clients ended up feeling like they were getting an even more intense workout in the remote coaching scenario.

And the remote coaching option created much-needed flexibility that helped clients fit working out into their lives. Christopherson believes that clients will want this kind of flexibility even as they move into a post-pandemic "new normal." An at-home option allows new parents to work out at home while the baby sleeps. Business travelers can keep up with remote coaching on their trips. And even leisure travelers can keep their wellness routines dialed in during their vacations.

Christopherson emphasizes the importance of two-way communication between clients and coaches. He believes that's what set his company apart from competitors that offered on-demand video workouts. "You need a dialogue, not a monologue, for optimizing workouts," he tells me. Their virtual fitness model, better defined as "remote coaching," brought accountability into clients' homes.

When their gym's doors opened back up in June 2020, Innovative Fitness was still laser-focused on understanding clients' needs. They surveyed their members and found that 49% of clients said they were ready to come back to the gym in person, while 26% wanted a hybrid option of both remote coaching and in-person workouts. Their customer experience model had to change, permanently, to provide more flexibility and freedom for their clients.

The question of what gyms and fitness will look like in the future will be in flux at least for a couple of years. Online workout options have proliferated, and gyms are seen as a high-risk environment, even as many places emerged from the most severe lockdown phase.[19] But I would bet on Christopherson and Innovative Fitness to succeed in this changing environment—because they're focusing so closely on creating a best-in-class customer experience no matter where they are.

Move forward in
a collaborative spirit.
Let them tell you
what they need, and
then **share how you
believe you can help
meet those needs**.

———————————————

The bar for convenience has been raised by the coronavirus experience. Consumer behavior in China, where lockdowns were imposed first and lifted first, offered some clues to what customers will want even going forward. Consumers in China stuck with trends like contactless delivery, cashless payments, and in-home options like telemedicine or remote learning even after the immediate threat of the virus had passed.[20]

At the same time, people want connection as much as, or even more than, they want efficiency. A 2020 survey by CGS looked at what people wanted from customer service during the coronavirus pandemic. They found that people wanted the option to speak to a human being, and they wanted that person to be friendly and resolve their problems quickly. It sounds simple, but it's an important reminder at a time when many companies are shifting a lot of their customer service resources into digital channels like chat and email: people want that human connection, particularly in times of crisis.[21]

I believe the future of the customer experience is a kind of hybrid model, where a high-touch, personalized experience of human connection is supported by digital technology that enables amazing convenience and efficiency. With today's tools, efficiency should be the easy part. It's the human connection part that demands your time and attention.

Value-added virtual experiences

Would you like to take a virtual bike tour with an Olympic cyclist? Learn the basics of K-beauty from a Korean television host and makeup artist? How about doing a Zoom meditation session with some real live sleepy sheep?

During the coronavirus pandemic, Airbnb launched an online version of its Experiences concept, so that people stuck at home could virtually travel and have unique experiences with hosts from around the world. And the company plans to keep these online experiences going post-pandemic, with the idea that hosts in popular tourist destinations can go virtual during their region's off-seasons to make extra cash. As one host who used to teach pasta-making classes in Florence, Italy, put it, "We realized that the world was changing, but not us. We do what we used to do before, still making connections, just in a different way."[22]

Airbnb isn't alone in trying to create an enticing virtual experience that recreates some of the joys of travel. Abu Dhabi's tourism industry was, of course, hit hard by the pandemic. So the city created a virtual Visit Abu Dhabi experience, complete with 360-degree videos, interactive tours of major sites, and first-person view drone videos that allow you to fly over sand dunes and through amazing architectural wonders.[23] These virtual experiences not only gave people something different to do during quarantine, but they also whetted the appetite for an in-person visit someday.

Right now, it's unclear when we'll be able to return to real-world travel and live, in-person events. But some innovative performers are going ahead with interesting new forms of live performance.

When the coronavirus lockdowns first started, many artists hosted free livestreaming performances. But the future of virtual events may be ticketed and limited, to generate more revenue for artists. Some performers have started experimenting with livestream shows with limited capacity, finding that creating a little scarcity helps make the event feel more exclusive and more exciting.[24] Keanu Reeves actually auctioned off a *very* exclusive live event—a 15-minute one-on-one Zoom call, with the proceeds going to a children's cancer charity.[25]

One virtual event platform said they'd seen 1,000% growth in the first few months of the pandemic.[26] People stuck in lockdowns were clearly craving virtual escapes. But online events weren't the only creative solution to the problems posed by the pandemic. The *Immersive van Gogh Exhibit* in Toronto, planned as a walk-in art exhibit that would project van Gogh's masterworks onto 15-meter-high walls and surround viewers with color and light, pivoted to become the world's first drive-in art exhibit.[27]

Of course, all these creative solutions have come out of dire necessity. People in the travel and entertainment industries have been forced to find alternatives to the live, in-person events they rely on for revenue. Post-pandemic, when a coronavirus vaccine is widely available and the threat is truly behind us, I would bet on in-person events to bounce back—perhaps even stronger than before, as people who've been quarantining on and off for months look for reasons to get out of the house.

But I believe some value-added virtual events pioneered during the pandemic will continue to draw viewers after the lockdowns are over. The key to drawing a virtual crowd when competing with in-person options will be understanding what makes a live event exciting, whether it's online, on television, or IRL.

Live experiences introduce randomness, intimacy, and absurdity into our lives. Remember my story about the Speedo bet? I know, I'm still traumatized too. That never would have happened if we'd been reading from a script. The best virtual events look nothing like a Zoom staff meeting—they take full advantage of the endless possibilities of the live-but-socially-distanced virtual world. One hot virtual gathering platform, High Fidelity, creates a three-dimensional audio experience, so participants can move through virtual space, hearing people's voices closer or farther away as they move.[28] Imagine attending a party inside the human body, where live performers take you through different experiences themed around different parts of the body: a concert in the ears, drawing exercises in the hands, a reflective rebirth experience in the womb.[29] Or what about a virtual hot tub, where participants are all in their own bathtubs at home?[30]

We will all be starved for connection when we finally leave the socially distanced lifestyle behind us for good. We'll flock back to in-person events. Some of those in-person experiences will have been fundamentally altered by the recession caused by the pandemic. Movie theaters, for example, are struggling financially right now, and some experts believe that major tech companies like Amazon might buy up those theater chains and create new kinds of event experiences or offer a certain number of real-world theater tickets as a bonus with streaming subscriptions.[31]

In this new post-pandemic world, the virtual experiences that stand out and keep drawing eyeballs will be the ones that capture the organic magic of a live experience—and use the limitless potential of the virtual world in creative ways. These value-added virtual experiences could continue bringing us together at a distance long after the pandemic has passed.

Back to the future

In some ways, our post-pandemic future will eventually look a lot like our past: we'll go back to gathering in groups. We'll watch live sports, live concerts, and live theater. We'll go to the movie theater. Many of us will go back to working in offices. Pandemics can't change human nature, and humans are social animals.

But pandemics do change human history. In many cases, pandemics have accelerated changes that were already building before a virus forced us to change our habits. In the case of coronavirus, I believe that the pandemic will accelerate the long-term trends that have been pushing us toward living in a half-virtual, half-real world. Many more people will work remotely post-pandemic than did before the coronavirus hit. Some conferences and other events will remain online, or offer livestreaming options, to be more accessible to people who can't travel to the in-person event. Many people will continue to take advantage of the convenience of virtual services like online fitness classes.

In this hybrid environment, the individuals and brands that succeed will put relationships first. Connection is paramount, whether you're connecting face-to-face or from a distance. Leaders will need to be more empathetic than ever before to motivate a far-flung remote workforce. Salespeople will need to lead with listening to meet customers where they are in a transformed world. Customer experience professionals will need to use all the technological tools at their disposal to create world-class convenience—and concentrate their resources on creating human connections. Events, whether physical or virtual, will need to put the organic, unpredictable live element front and center to draw an audience.

We humans will always crave connection. Keep that in the front of your mind, and you'll be able to navigate whatever change is coming your way.

CONCLUSION

"CALL HOME"

T HE FINAL text message from Dad that I have saved in my phone is just two simple, yet familiar, words: "call home." I look at these words often, knowing that hearing his voice is a luxury I no longer have. I received that message weeks before the most difficult phone call of my life.

In October of 2019, I was in a session at a conference with my brother Zain in San Diego, so I let the initial call go to voice mail. Ten minutes later, I listened to the message and heard sheer panic in Mom's voice. She could barely get through the words to say that something had happened to Dad. I could hear paramedics in the background using a defibrillator trying to revive him.

I immediately called home. Mom picked up the phone. I still could barely make out her words through her breathing and state of shock. I understood that Dad had stopped breathing and that Mom was headed to the hospital with our neighbor. I hung up, looked at Zain, and told him, "We need to go home."

We took the first flight back to Vancouver. When we arrived at Surrey Memorial Hospital later that evening, a lot of our family was thankfully already there, supporting both Dad and Mom.

Dad was lying in his room, unconscious, breathing with the ventilator. Seeing him like that was like a punch to the gut.

When the doctor came to check in, he pulled us aside and privately gave us an update: "Your father's heart stopped this morning. Paramedics were able to revive him and get a pulse. But his brain was without oxygen for an extended period of time. We're cooling his body for 24 hours and then will warm him up and do a CT scan to determine the damage."

He relayed this devastating news swiftly, yet with powerful compassion. It all felt surreal. I do remember the doctor then stopped talking. The ensuing silence was deafening. But it was also so important. He gave us time to process and then allowed us to ask as many questions as we wanted. The doctor was direct, patient, and assertively empathetic. He knew our lives were about to change forever.

Twenty-four hours later, our new reality was clear. Dad's brain damage was too severe and he wouldn't regain consciousness. The only decision we had to make was when to take him off life support. On Sunday afternoon, October 13, 2019, surrounded by family, we said goodbye.

I have never cried the way I did on that drive home. A couple of months after his passing, someone shared with me that "death is a date on the calendar. But grief... grief is the calendar." These words couldn't be more true.

If there's one thing I'd want you to know about Dad, it's that he knew how to make people feel safe. I later discovered he had one English-language CD that he listened to in his car. It was Whitney Houston's *I Look to You* album. My first thought was, "Dad liked Whitney??" Funny thing is, I looked to him for many things. And he always looked at others and didn't just make them feel safe, but also made them feel like a "Million Dollar Bill." That's Track One on the album.

It is easy to take for granted that we're going to have an infinite number of conversations with the people who matter to us. What if I told you your time was up and you had the opportunity to have one final conversation with someone? Who would you reach out to? What would you say? Does that person even know how you're feeling right now? If not, what are you waiting for?

We have the opportunity to build real relationships in every single conversation. That conversation could change someone's life. Maybe yours. Don't hold back. Connect. The people in your life might be looking to you for more than you think. And no matter how big your distractions become, never miss out on your chance to call home.

NOTES

Introduction: Look at You vs. Look at Me

1 Sebastian Junger, *Tribe: On Homecoming and Belonging* (New York, NY: Grand Central Publishing, 2016).

2 John F. Helliwell and Haifang Huang, "Comparing the Happiness Effects of Real and On-Line Friends," *PLoS One* 8, no. 9 (2013): doi.org/10.1371/journal.pone.0072754.

The Social Pandemic

1 LeBron James (@KingJames), Twitter post, March 11, 2020, 10:24 p.m., twitter.com/kingjames/status/1237972755275870208?lang=en.

2 Bonnie Evie Gifford, "Working from Home Taking a Toll on Our Mental Health and Relationships," *Happiful Magazine*, June 18, 2020, happiful.com/working-from-home-taking-toll-on-mental-health-relationships/; Ted Michaels, "Many Canadians Dealing with Mental Health Issues Due to Coronavirus: Survey," Global News, June 23, 2020, globalnews.ca/news/7092929/coronavirus-mental-health-canada/; Tamara Lush, "Poll: Americans Are the Unhappiest They've Been in 50 Years," Associated Press, June 16, 2020, apnews.com/0f6b9be04fa0d3194401821a72665a50; Elke Van Hoof, "Lockdown Is the World's Biggest Psychological Experiment—And We Will Pay the Price," World Economic Forum, April 9, 2020, weforum.org/agenda/2020/04/this-is-the-psychological-side-of-the-covid-19-pandemic-that-were-ignoring/.

3 Tim Adams, "Interview: John Cacioppo: 'Loneliness Is Like an Iceberg—It Goes Deeper Than We Can See,'" *The Guardian*, February 28, 2016, theguardian.com/science/2016/feb/28/loneliness-is-like-an-iceberg-john-cacioppo-social-neuroscience-interview.

4 Vivek Murthy, *Together: The Healing Power of Human Connection in a Sometimes Lonely World* (New York, NY: Harper Wave, 2020).

5   Bianca DiJulio et al., "Loneliness and Social Isolation in the United States, the United Kingdom, and Japan: An International Survey," Kaiser Family Foundation, August 30, 2018, kff.org/report-section/loneliness-and-social-isolation-in-the-united-states-the-united-kingdom-and-japan-an-international-survey-introduction/; David Frank, "1 in 3 U.S. Adults Are Lonely, Survey Shows," AARP, September 26, 2018, aarp.org/home-family/friends-family/info-2018/loneliness-survey.html; Ellie Polack, "New Cigna Study Reveals Loneliness at Epidemic Levels in America," Cigna, May 1, 2018, cigna.com/newsroom/news-releases/2018/new-cigna-study-reveals-loneliness-at-epidemic-levels-in-america; Perlita Stroh, "Feeling Lonely? You're Not Alone— And It Could Be Affecting Your Physical Health," CBC News, January 19, 2019, cbc.ca/news/health/national-dealing-with-loneliness-1.4828017; "Loneliness Research," Campaign to End Loneliness, campaigntoendloneliness.org/loneliness-research/; "Japan's 'Hikikomori' Population Could Top 10 Million," Nippon.com, September 17, 2020, nippon.com/en/japan-topics/c05008/japan%E2%80%99s-hikikomori-population-could-top-10-million.html.

6   "13 Words You Probably Didn't Know Were Invented by Shakespeare," *Huff-Post*, December 6, 2017, huffpost.com/entry/shakespeare-words_n_4590819; Josh Jones, "The 1,700+ Words Invented by Shakespeare*," *Open Culture*, April 2, 2018, openculture.com/2018/04/the-1700-words-invented-by-shakespeare.html; William Shakespeare, *Coriolanus*, Act IV, scene iii, lines 2552–54, available at *OpenSourceShakespeare*, opensourceshakespeare.org/views/plays/play_view.php?WorkID=coriolanus&Act=4&Scene=3&Scope=scene.

7   Murthy, *Together*.

8   Ellen Byron, "More Americans Are Living Solo, and Companies Want Their Business," *Wall Street Journal*, June 2, 2019, wsj.com/articles/more-americans-are-living-solo-and-companies-want-their-business-11559497606.

9   Eli Rosenberg, "Workers Are Fired Up. But Union Participation Is Still on the Decline, New Statistics Show," *Washington Post*, January 23, 2020, washingtonpost.com/business/2020/01/22/workers-are-fired-up-union-participation-is-still-decline-new-statistics-show/.

10   "In U.S., Decline of Christianity Continues at Rapid Pace," Pew Research Center, October 17, 2019, pewforum.org/2019/10/17/in-u-s-decline-of-christianity-continues-at-rapid-pace/.

11   Drew DeSilver, "For Most U.S. Workers, Real Wages Have Barely Budged in Decades," Pew Research Center, August 7, 2018, pewresearch.org/fact-tank/2018/08/07/for-most-us-workers-real-wages-have-barely-budged-for-decades/.

12   Preeti Malani and John Piette, "Loneliness and Health," National Poll on Healthy Aging, March 4, 2019, healthyagingpoll.org/report/loneliness-and-health; Donald Redfoot et al., "The Aging of the Baby Boom and the Growing Care Gap: A Look at Future Declines in the Availability of Family Caregivers," AARP Public Policy Institute, August 2013, aarp.org/content/dam/aarp/research/public_policy_institute/ltc/2013/baby-boom-and-the-growing-care-gap-insight-AARP-ppi-ltc.pdf.

13 Jason Rhode, "LGBTQ Seniors Face Unique Challenges," *Georgia Voice*, May 1, 2018, thegavoice.com/community/features/lgbtq-seniors-face-unique-challenges/.

14 "The Number of International Migrants Reaches 272 Million, Continuing an Upward Trend in all World Regions, Says UN," United Nations Department of Economic and Social Affairs, September 17, 2019, un.org/development/desa/en/news/population/international-migrant-stock-2019.html.

15 Katrina Trinko, "Gen Z Is the Loneliest Generation, and It's Not Just Because of Social Media," *USA Today*, May 3, 2018, usatoday.com/story/opinion/2018/05/03/gen-z-loneliest-generation-social-media-personal-interactions-column/574701002/.

16 "The Link between Loneliness and Technology," *Monitor on Psychology* 50, no. 5 (May 2019): apa.org/monitor/2019/05/ce-corner-sidebar.

17 Stephen Marche, "Is Facebook Making Us Lonely?" *The Atlantic*, May 2012, theatlantic.com/magazine/archive/2012/05/is-facebook-making-us-lonely/308930/.

18 Murthy, *Together*.

19 Manyu Jiang, "The Reason Zoom Calls Drain Your Energy," BBC, April 22, 2020, bbc.com/worklife/article/20200421-why-zoom-video-chats-are-so-exhausting.

20 Emily Esfahani Smith, "Social Connection Makes a Better Brain," *The Atlantic*, October 29, 2013, theatlantic.com/health/archive/2013/10/social-connection-makes-a-better-brain/280934/.

21 Murthy, *Together*.

22 Max McClure, "Infants Process Faces Long before They Recognize Other Objects, Stanford Vision Researchers Find," Stanford University, December 11, 2012, news.stanford.edu/news/2012/december/infants-process-faces-121112.html.

23 Jason M. Breslow, "What Does Solitary Confinement Do to Your Mind?" PBS, April 22, 2014, pbs.org/wgbh/frontline/article/what-does-solitary-confinement-do-to-your-mind/.

24 Murthy, *Together*.

25 Ibid.

26 Eli J. Finkel and Paul W. Eastwick, "Speed-Dating," *Current Directions in Psychological Science* 17, no. 3 (2008): doi.org/10.1111/j.1467-8721.2008.00573.x.

27 Andrea Petersen, "The Surprising Science behind Friendship," *Wall Street Journal*, February 9, 2020, wsj.com/articles/the-surprising-science-behind-friendship-11581256802.

28 Jamie Friedlander, "How Small Talk with Almost-Strangers Profoundly Affects Your Happiness," *Vice*, May 7, 2019, vice.com/en_us/article/kzmb43/how-small-talk-with-almost-strangers-profoundly-affects-your-happiness.

29 Adams, "Interview: John Cacioppo."

30 Stephanie Watson, "Volunteering May Be Good for Body and Mind," *Harvard HEALTHbeat*, June 26, 2013, health.harvard.edu/blog/volunteering-may-be-good-for-body-and-mind-201306266428.

Listen without Distraction

1   Ralph G. Nichols and Leonard A. Stevens, "Listening to People," *Harvard Business Review*, September 1957, hbr.org/1957/09/listening-to-people.

2   Bob Sullivan and Hugh Thompson, "Now Hear This! Most People Stink at Listening [Excerpt]," *Scientific American*, May 3, 2013, scientificamerican.com/article/plateau-effect-digital-gadget-distraction-attention/.

3   Nadia Whitehead, "People Would Rather Be Electrically Shocked Than Left Alone with Their Thoughts," *Science*, July 3, 2014, sciencemag.org/news/2014/07/people-would-rather-be-electrically-shocked-left-alone-their-thoughts.

4   Sullivan and Thompson, "Now Hear This!"

5   Stephanie Vozza, "6 Ways to Become a Better Listener," *Fast Company*, March 17, 2017), fastcompany.com/3068959/6-ways-to-become-a-better-listener.

6   Thomas Oppong, "The Psychology of Thinking vs. Doing," *Thrive Global*, February 5, 2018, thriveglobal.com/stories/the-psychology-of-thinking-vs-doing/.

7   Nichols and Stevens, "Listening to People."

8   Sullivan and Thompson, "Now Hear This!"; Kenneth Miller, "How Our Ancient Brains Are Coping in the Age of Digital Distraction," *Discover Magazine*, April 20, 2020, discovermagazine.com/mind/how-our-ancient-brains-are-coping-in-the-age-of-digital-distraction; "Information Addiction: How Information Is Like Snacks, Money, and Drugs to Your Brain," *Neuroscience News*, June 19, 2019, neurosciencenews.com/information-addiction-brain-14274/.

9   Sullivan and Thompson, "Now Hear This!"

10 "Americans Check Their Phones 96 Times a Day," PR Newswire, November 21, 2019, prnewswire.com/news-releases/americans-check-their-phones-96-times-a-day-300962643.html; Miller, "How Our Ancient Brains Are Coping"; "Distracted Driving 2015," U.S. Department of Transportation, National Highway Traffic Safety Administration, March 2017, nhtsa.gov/sites/nhtsa.dot.gov/files/documents/812_381_distracteddriving2015.pdf; Daniel C. Smith et al., "Ambulatory Cell Phone Injuries in the United States: An Emerging National Concern," *Journal of Safety Research* 47 (2013): doi.org/10.1016/j.jsr.2013.08.003.

11 Steve Corona, "How 30 Days without Social Media Changed My Life," *SteveCorona* (blog), accessed July 22, 2020, stevecorona.com/how-30-days-without-social-media-changed-my-life.

12 Megan Cerullo, "Most Americans Check in at Work Even While on Vacation, LinkedIn Survey Shows," CBS News, July 10, 2019, cbsnews.com/news/most-americans-check-work-email-while-on-vacation-linkedin-survey/; Clive Thompson, "Are You Checking Work Email in Bed? At the Dinner Table? On Vacation?" *Mother Jones*, May/June 2014, motherjones.com/politics/2014/04/smartphone-addiction-research-work-email/.

13 Shunryu Suzuki, *Zen Mind, Beginner's Mind* (Boulder, CO: Shambhala Publications, 2006).

14 Jack Zenger and Joseph Folkman, "What Great Listeners Actually Do," *Harvard Business Review*, July 14, 2016, hbr.org/2016/07/ what-great-listeners-actually-do.

Make Your Small Talk Bigger

1 Paul Ingram and Michael W. Morris, "Do People Mix at Mixers? Structure, Homophily, and the 'Life of the Party,'" *Administrative Science Quarterly* 52, no. 4 (2007): doi.org/10.2189/asqu.52.4.558; Susan Adams, "Why You Hate Networking," *Forbes*, September 16, 2014, forbes.com/sites/susanadams/2014/ 09/16/why-you-hate-networking/; Gina Belli, "How Many Jobs Are Found through Networking, Really?" PayScale, April 6, 2017, payscale.com/career-news/2017/04/many-jobs-found-networking.

2 Jennifer K. South Palomares and Andrew W. Young, "Facial First Impressions of Partner Preference Traits: Trustworthiness, Status, and Attractiveness," *Social Psychology and Personality Science* 9, no. 8 (2018): doi.org/10.1177/ 1948550617732388; Mark Rowh, "First Impressions Count," *gradPSYCH* 10, no. 4 (2012): apa.org/gradpsych/2012/11/first-impressions.

3 Don Peppers, "There Are 2 Kinds of Curiosity. Only One of Them Is Good for Your Business," *Inc.*, April 26, 2018, inc.com/linkedin/don-peppers/do-you-have-right-kind-curiosity-don-peppers.html.

4 Mario Livio (interview), "The 'Why' behind Asking Why: The Science of Curiosity," *Knowledge@Wharton* (podcast), August 23, 2017, knowledge. wharton.upenn.edu/article/makes-us-curious/.

5 Christopher Bergland, "Curiosity: The Good, the Bad, and the Double-Edged Sword," *Psychology Today*, August 4, 2016, psychologytoday.com/ca/blog/the-athletes-way/201608/curiosity-the-good-the-bad-and-the-double-edged-sword.

6 Emily Campbell, "Six Surprising Benefits of Curiosity," *Greater Good Magazine*, September 24, 2015, greatergood.berkeley.edu/article/item/six_ surprising_benefits_of_curiosity; Markham Heid, "Curiosity Is the Secret to a Happy Life," *Medium*, February 13, 2020, elemental.medium.com/curiosity-is-the-secret-to-a-happy-life-3dc5d940d602.

7 Francesca Gino, "The Business Case for Curiosity," *Harvard Business Review*, September/October 2018, hbr.org/2018/09/curiosity.

8 Todd B. Kashdan et al., "Curiosity Protects against Interpersonal Aggression: Cross-Sectional, Daily Process, and Behavioral Evidence," *Journal of Personality* 81, no. 1 (2013): doi.org/10.1111/j.1467-6494.2012.00783.x; Todd B. Kashdan and John E. Roberts, "Affective Outcomes in Superficial and Intimate Interactions: Roles of Social Anxiety and Curiosity," *Journal of Research in Personality* 40, no. 2 (2006): doi.org/10.1016/j.jrp.2004.10.005; Taishi Kawamoto et al., "Curious People Are Less Affected by Social Rejection," *Personality and Individual Differences* 105 (2017): doi.org/10.1016/j.paid.2016.10.006.

9 Jill Suttie, "Why Curious People Have Better Relationships," *Greater Good Magazine*, May 31, 2017, greatergood.berkeley.edu/article/item/why_curious_ people_have_better_relationships; Todd B. Kashdan et al., "When Curiosity

Breeds Intimacy: Taking Advantage of Intimacy Opportunities and Transforming Boring Conversations," *Journal of Personality* 79, no. 6 (2011): doi.org/10.1111/j.1467-6494.2010.00697.x; Todd B. Kashdan and John E. Roberts, "Trait and State Curiosity in the Genesis of Intimacy: Differentiation from Related Constructs," *Journal of Social and Clinical Psychology* 23, no. 6 (2004): doi.org/10.1521/jscp.23.6.792.54800.

10   "John Ratzenberger," Pixar Wiki, accessed July 22, 2020, pixar.fandom.com/wiki/John_Ratzenberger.

11   Ian Leslie, "Don't Let Curiosity Be Killed by Cats," *Wired*, August 24, 2015, wired.co.uk/article/dont-let-curiosity-be-killed-by-cats.

12   Tim Wu, "The Tyranny of Convenience," *New York Times*, February 16, 2018, nytimes.com/2018/02/16/opinion/sunday/tyranny-convenience.html.

13   Livio, "The 'Why' behind Asking Why."

14   Jud Brewer, "A 10-Second Eye Exercise to Calm Your Mind," *Medium*, April 28, 2020, elemental.medium.com/a-10-second-eye-exercise-to-calm-your-mind-2f1bb208a28.

15   Stephanie Vozza, "8 Habits of Curious People," *Fast Company*, April 21, 2015, fastcompany.com/3045148/8-habits-of-curious-people.

16   Carly Stec, "How to Be a More Curious Person: 7 Tips for Becoming a Lifelong Learner," HubSpot, January 7, 2016, blog.hubspot.com/marketing/be-more-curious-tips.

17   Bernadette Jiwa, "8 Ways to Unleash Your Curiosity," *Success*, June 8, 2017, success.com/8-ways-to-unleash-your-curiosity/.

18   Daniel Jones, "The 36 Questions That Lead to Love," *New York Times*, January 9, 2015, nytimes.com/2015/01/11/style/36-questions-that-lead-to-love.html.

19   Gino, "The Business Case for Curiosity"; Diane Hamilton, "How to Instill Curiosity in the Workplace," *Forbes*, April 3, 2020, forbes.com/sites/forbescoachescouncil/2020/04/03/how-to-instill-curiosity-in-the-workplace/.

20   Petrana Radulovic, "How the '20% Time' Rule Led to Google's Most Innovative Products," *Mashable*, May 11, 2018, mashable.com/2018/05/11/google-20-percent-rule/.

21   Hal Gregersen, "Better Brainstorming," *Harvard Business Review*, March/April 2018, hbr.org/2018/03/better-brainstorming.

22   Christine Carter, "7 Ways to Foster Creativity in Your Kids," *Greater Good Magazine*, September 16, 2008, greatergood.berkeley.edu/article/item/7_ways_to_foster_creativity_in_your_kids; "Creativity and Play: Fostering Creativity," PBS, accessed July 22, 2020, pbs.org/wholechild/providers/play.html; Maria Onzain, "13 Ways to Encourage Curiosity in Children That Most Parents Ignore," *Lifehack*, August 3, 2016, lifehack.org/444453/13-ways-to-encourage-curiosity-in-children-that-most-parents-ignore; Michael Kress, "11 Tips to Encourage Curiosity," *Highlights*, April 19, 2016, highlights.com/parents/articles/11-tips-encourage-curiosity.

23 Peter Bregman, "Empathy Starts with Curiosity," *Harvard Business Review*, April 27, 2020, hbr.org/2020/04/empathy-starts-with-curiosity?ab=hero-subleft-1.

24 Dave Stubbs, "Bobby Orr: 100 Greatest NHL Players," NHL.com, January 1, 2017, nhl.com/news/bobby-orr-100-greatest-nhl-hockey-players/c-285636896?tid=283865022.

25 Greg Toppo, "Self-Help Guru Wayne W. Dyer Dies at 75," *USA Today*, August 30, 2015, usatoday.com/story/life/people/2015/08/30/wayne-dyer-obituary/71435806/.

Put Aside Your Perfect Persona

1 Aidan McCullen, "Removing the Mask—Self Alignment," *Medium*, October 3, 2018, medium.com/thethursdaythought/removing-the-mask-self-alignment-cd27bb91e619.

2 Laurie Leinwand, "The Masks We Wear: Could They Be Good for Us?" *GoodTherapy* (blog), October 20, 2015, goodtherapy.org/blog/masks-we-wear-could-they-be-good-for-us-1020155.

3 Kim Elsesser, "Power Posing Is Back: Amy Cuddy Successfully Refutes Criticism," *Forbes*, April 3, 2018, forbes.com/sites/kimelsesser/2018/04/03/power-posing-is-back-amy-cuddy-successfully-refutes-criticism/.

4 Mary Retta, "The Mental Health Cost of Code-Switching on Campus," *Teen Vogue*, September 18, 2019, teenvogue.com/story/the-mental-health-cost-of-code-switching-on-campus.

5 Joseph Stromberg, "Coming Out of the Closet May Be Good for Your Health," *Smithsonian Magazine*, January 29, 2013, smithsonianmag.com/science-nature/coming-out-of-the-closet-may-be-good-for-your-health-7400182/.

6 Lisa Marie Bobby, "How to Be More Vulnerable in Relationships," Growing Self Counseling & Coaching, February 26, 2020, growingself.com/how-to-be-more-vulnerable-in-relationships/.

7 Ashley Boucher, "Kaitlyn Bristowe Opens Up about Previous Valium Addiction When She Weighed Just 93 Pounds," *People*, May 6, 2020, people.com/health/kaitlyn-bristowe-opens-up-previous-valium-addiction-weighed-93-pounds/.

8 Alice G. Walton, "Jealous of Your Facebook Friends? Why Social Media Makes Us Bitter," *Forbes*, January 23, 2013, forbes.com/sites/alicegwalton/2013/01/22/jealous-of-your-facebook-friends-why-social-media-makes-us-bitter/.

9 Mai-Ly N. Steers et al., "Seeing Everyone Else's Highlight Reels: How Facebook Usage Is Linked to Depressive Symptoms," *Journal of Social and Clinical Psychology* 33, no. 8 (2014): doi.org/10.1521/jscp.2014.33.8.701.

10 "*Election* (1999)," IMDb, accessed July 22, 2020, imdb.com/title/tt0126886/characters/nm0000702.

11   Jackie Vandinther, "Showing Emotion No Longer Taboo for Political Leaders during Pandemic," CTV News, May 5, 2020, ctvnews.ca/health/coronavirus/showing-emotion-no-longer-taboo-for-political-leaders-during-pandemic-1.4925464; Roy Peter Clark, "'It's OK to Not Be OK Right Now.' TV Anchors Are Setting aside the Stoicism and Getting Personal," *Poynter*, May 13, 2020, poynter.org/ethics-trust/2020/its-ok-to-not-be-ok-right-now-tv-anchors-are-setting-aside-the-stoicism-and-getting-personal/.

12   "JFK Assassination: Cronkite Informs a Shocked Nation," CBS Sunday Morning, YouTube (video), 1:50, November 17, 2013, youtube.com/watch?v=6PXORQE5-CY; "JFK Assassination," Walter Cronkite: The Most Trusted Man in America, University of Oregon Media by the Decades Project, accessed July 22, 2020, blogs.uoregon.edu/frengsj387/jfk-assassination/.

13   Emily Esfahani Smith, "Your Flaws Are Probably More Attractive Than You Think They Are," *The Atlantic*, January 9, 2019, theatlantic.com/health/archive/2019/01/beautiful-mess-vulnerability/579892/.

14   Alison Wood Brooks et al., "Smart People Ask for (My) Advice: Seeking Advice Boosts Perceptions of Competence," *Management Science* 61, no. 6 (2015): dx.doi.org/10.1287/mnsc.2014.2054.

15   Brené Brown, *I Thought It Was Just Me: Women Reclaiming Power and Courage in a Culture of Shame* (West Hollywood, CA: Gotham Books, 2007); "Courage (n.)," *Online Etymology Dictionary*, accessed July 22, 2020, etymonline.com/word/courage.

16   Emma Seppälä, "The Real Secret to Intimacy (and Why It Scares Us)," *Psychology Today*, September 5, 2012, psychologytoday.com/us/blog/feeling-it/201209/the-real-secret-intimacy-and-why-it-scares-us; "Lying Less Linked to Better Health, New Research Finds," American Psychological Association (press release), 2012, apa.org/news/press/releases/2012/08/lying-less.

17   Esfahani Smith, "Your Flaws Are Probably More Attractive Than You Think."

18   Andy Chan, "Here's How a Leader's Vulnerability Backfires," *Medium*, December 14, 2019, medium.com/the-human-business/heres-how-a-leader-s-vulnerability-backfires-df91814f7230.

19   Brené Brown, *Daring Greatly: How the Courage to Be Vulnerable Transforms the Way We Live, Love, Parent, and Lead* (West Hollywood, GA: Gotham Books, 2012).

20   Justin Bariso, "Neuroscience Shows Psychopaths Can Use Emotional Intelligence to Harm. Here's How to Protect Yourself," *Inc.*, July 25, 2018, inc.com/justin-bariso/neuroscience-shows-psychopaths-can-use-emotional-intelligence-to-harm-heres-how-to-protect-yourself.html.

21   Alice Williams, "When Vulnerability Backfires," *Daily Life*, June 16, 2014, dailylife.com.au/news-and-views/dl-opinion/when-vulnerability-backfires-20140613-3a2cy.html; Hannah Braime, "Vulnerability vs. Over-Sharing: Where to Draw the Line?" *Becoming Who You Are* (blog), February 11, 2013, becomingwhoyouare.net/blog/vulnerability-vs-over-sharing-where-to-draw-the-line.

22 John C. Maxwell, *Everyone Communicates, Few Connect: What the Most Effective People Do Differently* (Nashville, TN: Thomas Nelson, 2010).

23 "Interesting Psychological Phenomena: The Pratfall Effect," Brescia University, June 26, 2017, brescia.edu/2017/06/pratfall-effect/.

Be Assertively Empathetic

1   Sarah Maslin Nir, "The Bird Watcher, That Incident and His Feelings on the Woman's Fate," *New York Times*, May 27, 2020, nytimes.com/2020/05/27/nyregion/amy-cooper-christian-central-park-video.html; Brakkton Booker, "Woman Who Called Police on Black Bird-Watcher in Central Park to Be Charged," NPR, July 6, 2020, npr.org/sections/live-updates-protests-for-racial-justice/2020/07/06/887809759/woman-who-called-police-on-black-bird-watcher-in-central-park-to-be-charged.

2   Raisa Bruner, "Michelle Obama Explains What 'Going High' Really Means," *Time*, November 20, 2018, time.com/5459984/michelle-obama-go-high/.

3   Emma Seppälä, "Empathy Is on the Decline in This Country. A New Book Describes What We Can Do to Bring It Back," *Washington Post*, June 11, 2019, washingtonpost.com/lifestyle/2019/06/11/empathy-is-decline-this-country-new-book-describes-what-we-can-do-bring-it-back/.

4   Jamil Zaki, "In a Divided World, We Need to Choose Empathy," *Greater Good Magazine*, May 29, 2019, greatergood.berkeley.edu/article/item/in_a_divided_world_we_need_to_choose_empathy.

5   Alan Martin, "Online Disinhibition and the Psychology of Trolling," *Wired*, May 30, 2013, wired.co.uk/article/online-aggression.

6   "Troll Patrol Findings: Using Crowdsourcing, Data Science & Machine Learning to Measure Violence and Abuse against Women on Twitter," Amnesty International, accessed July 22, 2020, decoders.amnesty.org/projects/troll-patrol/findings.

7   Adeel Hassan, "Hate-Crime Violence Hits 16-Year High, F.B.I. Reports," *New York Times*, November 12, 2019, nytimes.com/2019/11/12/us/hate-crimes-fbi-report.html.

8   Amber Lee, "Professor Tracks Racism against Asian Americans during COVID-19," FOX 10 Phoenix, May 19, 2020, fox10phoenix.com/news/professor-tracks-racism-against-asian-americans-during-covid-19; Simon Little and John Hua, "New Campaign Urges Canadians to Speak Up amid Surge in Anti-Asian Racism," Global News, May 22, 2020, globalnews.ca/news/6977278/coronavirus-anti-racism-campaign/.

9   Dylan Scott, "Covid-19's Devastating Toll on Black and Latino Americans, in One Chart," *Vox*, April 17, 2020, vox.com/2020/4/17/21225610/us-coronavirus-death-rates-blacks-latinos-whites; Lipi Roy, "COVID-19 Testing in Homeless Shelters: Care, Compassion and Combatting Structural Inequalities," *Forbes*, May 4, 2020, forbes.com/sites/lipiroy/2020/05/04/covid-19-testing-in-homeless-shelters-care-compassion-and-combatting-structural-inequalities/.

10 Evan Hill et al., "How George Floyd Was Killed in Police Custody," *New York Times*, May 31, 2020, nytimes.com/2020/05/31/us/george-floyd-investigation.html; Charlotte Alter, "'America Has Its Knee on People of Color.' Why George Floyd's Death Was a Breaking Point," *Time*, May 31, 2020, time.com/5845752/america-has-its-knee-on-us-george-floyds-death-was-a-breaking-point-protests/; Larry Buchanan et al., "Black Lives Matter May Be the Largest Movement in U.S. History," *New York Times*, July 3, 2020, nytimes.com/interactive/2020/07/03/us/george-floyd-protests-crowd-size.html; Jen Kirby, "'Black Lives Matter' Has Become a Global Rallying Cry against Racism and Police Brutality," *Vox*, June 12, 2020, vox.com/2020/6/12/21285244/black-lives-matter-global-protests-george-floyd-uk-belgium.

11 Clare Malone and Kyle Bourassa, "Americans Didn't Wait for Their Governors to Tell Them to Stay Home Because of COVID-19," *FiveThirtyEight*, May 8, 2020, fivethirtyeight.com/features/americans-didnt-wait-for-their-governors-to-tell-them-to-stay-home-because-of-covid-19/.

12 David Enrich et al., "A Sewing Army, Making Masks for America," *New York Times*, March 25, 2020, nytimes.com/2020/03/25/business/coronavirus-masks-sewers.html.

13 Catherine Porter, "The Top Doctor Who Aced the Coronavirus Test," *New York Times*, June 5, 2020, nytimes.com/2020/06/05/world/canada/bonnie-henry-british-columbia-coronavirus.html.

14 Chris Megerian and Eli Stokols, "Trump Rarely Shows Empathy in Coronavirus Crisis," *Los Angeles Times*, May 4, 2020, latimes.com/world-nation/story/2020-05-04/trump-rarely-shows-empathy-in-coronavirus-crisis.

15 Eric Lipton et al., "He Could Have Seen What Was Coming: Behind Trump's Failure on the Virus," *New York Times*, April 11, 2020, nytimes.com/2020/04/11/us/politics/coronavirus-trump-response.html.

16 Shaimaa Khalil, "Coronavirus: How New Zealand Relied on Science and Empathy," BBC News, April 20, 2020, bbc.com/news/world-asia-52344299; Uri Friedman, "New Zealand's Prime Minister May Be the Most Effective Leader on the Planet," *The Atlantic*, April 19, 2020, theatlantic.com/politics/archive/2020/04/jacinda-ardern-new-zealand-leadership-coronavirus/610237/.

17 Anna Fifield, "New Zealand Edges Back to Normal after Quashing Coronavirus in 49 Days," *Washington Post*, May 16, 2020, washingtonpost.com/world/asia_pacific/new-zealand-edges-back-to-normal-after-routing-coronavirus-in-49-days/2020/05/15/c8f43f46-950e-11ea-87a3-22d324235636_story.html.

18 Haley Sweetland Edwards, "There Are Sensible Ways to Reopen a Country. Then There's America's Approach," *Time*, May 14, 2020, time.com/5836607/reopening-risks-coronavirus/.

19 Aaron Blake, "Forty-Nine of 50 Governors Have Better Coronavirus Poll Numbers Than Trump," *The Independent*, May 19, 2020, independent.co.uk/news/world/americas/us-politics/coronavirus-us-trump-poll-numbers-brian-kemp-a9522286.html.

20 Carlie Porterfield, "New Zealand's Female PM Is Most Popular Leader in a
Century as Country Goes Days with No Cases," *Forbes*, May 19, 2020, forbes.
com/sites/carlieporterfield/2020/05/19/new-zealands-female-pm-is-most-
popular-leader-in-a-century-as-country-goes-days-with-no-cases/.

21 Jamil Zaki, "The Technology of Kindness: How Social Media Can Rebuild
Our Empathy—And Why It Must," *Scientific American*, August 6, 2019,
scientificamerican.com/article/the-technology-of-kindness/; William J.
Brady et al., "Emotion Shapes the Diffusion of Moralized Content in Social
Networks," *Proceedings of the National Academy of Sciences* 114 no. 28 (2017):
doi.org/10.1073/pnas.1618923114.

22 "Find Social Media Frustrating? Try Empathy," University of California
Newsroom, February 11, 2020, universityofcalifornia.edu/news/
social-media-making-you-frustrated-try-empathy.

23 Drew Magary, "Sarah Silverman Is the Troll Slayer," *GQ*, May 23, 2018,
gq.com/story/sarah-silverman-i-love-you-america-profile; Allison Klein, "A
Sexist Troll Attacked Sarah Silverman. She Responded by Helping Him with
His Problems," *Washington Post*, January 8, 2018, washingtonpost.com/news/
inspired-life/wp/2018/01/08/a-man-trolled-sarah-silverman-on-twitter-she-
ended-up-helping-him-with-his-medical-problems/.

24 Kate Neilson, "People Will Do Anything to Avoid a Tough Conversation,
Even Quit," HRM/Australian HR Institute, October 21, 2019, hrmonline.com.
au/topics/management-of-workplace-issues/avoid-tough-conversation-quit/;
Kathy Gurchiek, "Tough Work Conversations Can Send People Running for
Cover," SHRM, October 17, 2019, shrm.org/resourcesandtools/hr-topics/
employee-relations/pages/tough-work-conversations-can-send-people-
running-for-cover.aspx; Michael Schneider, "Most People Handle Difficult
Situations by Ignoring Them—And the Fallout Isn't Pretty," *Inc.*, August 22,
2018, inc.com/michael-schneider/70-percent-of-employees-avoid-difficult-
conversations-their-companies-are-suffering-as-a-result.html.

25 Karen Gilchrist, "7 In 10 Americans Are Avoiding Difficult Conversations at
Work—Here's How to Tackle Them," CNBC, March 13, 2019, cnbc.com/
2019/03/14/how-to-deal-with-difficult-conversations-colleagues-at-work.html.

26 Carol Pavlish et al., "A Culture of Avoidance: Voices from inside Ethically
Difficult Clinical Situations," *Clinical Journal of Oncology Nursing* 19, no. 2
(2015): doi.org/10.1188/15.CJON.19-02AP.

27 Stephen Stubben and Kyle Welch, "Research: Whistleblowers Are a Sign of
Healthy Companies," *Harvard Business Review*, November 14, 2018, hbr.org/
2018/11/research-whistleblowers-are-a-sign-of-healthy-companies.

28 Chelsea Frisbie, "80% of Millennials Have Been 'Ghosted,' Survey Finds,"
Mashable, March 28, 2016, mashable.com/2016/03/28/ghosting-dating/.

29 Natalia Lusinski, "If You're Avoiding Having These 9 Conversations with Your
Partner, It May Be Time to Break Up," *Bustle*, May 2, 2018, bustle.com/p/if-
youre-avoiding-these-conversations-with-your-partner-it-may-be-time-to-
break-up-8964741.

30 Susie Steiner, "Top Five Regrets of the Dying," *The Guardian*, February 1, 2012, theguardian.com/lifeandstyle/2012/feb/01/top-five-regrets-of-the-dying.

31 Melody Wilding, "7 Habits of Highly Empathetic People," *Inc.*, January 7, 2019, inc.com/melody-wilding/7-habits-of-highly-empathetic-people.html.

32 Jessica Stillman, "3 Habits That Will Increase Your Empathy," *Inc.*, August 22, 2014, inc.com/jessica-stillman/3-habits-that-will-increase-your-empathy.html.

33 Sam Biederman and Emanuele Castano, "Reading Literary Fiction Improves 'Mind-Reading' Skills Finds a Study from the New School for Social Research," The New School (press release), October 3, 2013, newschool.edu/pressroom/pressreleases/2013/CastanoKidd.htm.

34 Claire Cain Miller, "How to Be More Empathetic," *New York Times*, accessed July 23, 2020, nytimes.com/guides/year-of-living-better/how-to-be-more-empathetic; Project Implicit, accessed July 23, 2020, implicit.harvard.edu/implicit/.

35 Rebecca Knight, "How to Develop Empathy for Someone Who Annoys You," *Harvard Business Review*, April 23, 2018, hbr.org/2018/04/how-to-develop-empathy-for-someone-who-annoys-you.

36 Jay Croft, "A Sheriff Put Down His Baton to Listen to Protesters. They Chanted 'Walk with Us,' So He Did," CNN, May 31, 2020, cnn.com/2020/05/31/us/flint-michigan-protest-police-trnd/index.html.

37 Knight, "How to Develop Empathy."

38 Hamid Dabashi, "The Salman Rushdie Affair: Thirty Years and a Novelist Later," *Al Jazeera*, February 18, 2019, aljazeera.com/indepth/opinion/salman-rushdie-affair-years-novelist-190217140017088.html.

39 Alan Manning and Nicole Amare, "Bad News First: How Optimal Directness Depends on What Is Negated," 2017 IEEE International Professional Communication Conference (July 23–26, Madison, WI), *Xplore* (August 24, 2017): doi.org/10.1109/IPCC.2017.8013959.

40 Leslie K. John et al., "Research Confirms: When Receiving Bad News, We Shoot the Messenger," *Harvard Business Review*, April 16, 2019, hbr.org/2019/04/research-confirms-when-receiving-bad-news-we-shoot-the-messenger.

41 Amy R. Overton and Ann C. Lowry, "Conflict Management: Difficult Conversations with Difficult People," *Clinics in Colon and Rectal Surgery* 26, no. 4 (2013): doi.org/10.1055/s-0033-1356728.

42 Elizabeth Svoboda, "Why Is It So Hard to Change People's Minds?" *Greater Good Magazine*, June 27, 2017, greatergood.berkeley.edu/article/item/why_is_it_so_hard_to_change_peoples_minds.

43 Céline Semaan, "Layla Saad Started an Instagram Challenge to Dismantle White Supremacy. Now It's a Best-Selling Book," *Elle*, December 7, 2018, elle.com/culture/career-politics/a25437280/layla-saad-me-and-white-supremacy-book/.

Make People Feel Famous

1 "Rick's Story," Rick Hansen Foundation, accessed July 23, 2020, rickhansen. com/about-rick/ricks-story; "Creating a World without Barriers," Rick Hansen Foundation, accessed July 23, 2020, rickhansen.com/about-us; "Man in Motion World Tour," Rick Hansen Foundation, accessed July 23, 2020, rickhansen.com/about-rick/man-motion-world-tour.

2 Rebecca Solnit, "Rebecca Solnit: How to Survive a Disaster," *Literary Hub*, November 15, 2016, lithub.com/rebecca-solnit-how-to-survive-a-disaster/.

3 Ryan Kelley, "America's First Responders' Struggle with PTSD and Depression," EMS1, October 28, 2019, emsi.com/ptsd/articles/americas-first-responders-struggle-with-ptsd-and-depression-LsgD4lAsb0ycVuQH/; Aaron Reuben, "When PTSD Is Contagious," *The Atlantic*, December 14, 2015, theatlantic.com/health/archive/2015/12/ptsd-secondary-trauma/420282/.

4 Emmy Schram et al., "Wellness in Emergency Medicine: The Importance of Gratitude during Times of Crisis," *Emergency Medicine Leader*, April 10, 2020, medicine.iu.edu/blogs/emergency-medicine-leader/the-importance-of-gratitude-during-times-of-crisis.

5 Eldis Sula, "5 Powerful Stories from Nurses on the Front Lines of COVID-19," Radio.com, May 12, 2020, radio.com/news/gallery/powerful-stories-from-nurses-on-the-front-lines-of-covid-19.

6 Andy Newman, "What N.Y.C. Sounds Like Every Night at 7," *New York Times*, April 10, 2020, nytimes.com/interactive/2020/04/10/nyregion/nyc-7pm-cheer-thank-you-coronavirus.html.

7 William Booth et al., "In Fight against Coronavirus, the World Gives Medical Heroes a Standing Ovation," *Washington Post*, March 26, 2020, washingtonpost.com/world/europe/clap-for-carers/2020/03/26/3d05eb9c-6f66-11ea-a156-0048b62adb51_story.html.

8 Angelina Walker, "This Compilation of Kind Words Written by Strangers, to Nurses, Will Make You Smile," Nurse.org, May 7, 2020, nurse.org/articles/nurse-appreciation-week-kind-words-quotes-support/.

9 Sula, "5 Powerful Stories from Nurses on the Front Lines."

10 "Banksy Drops Off Superhero Nurse Artwork at Hospital in UK with a Thank You Note," Good News Network, May 8, 2020, goodnewsnetwork.org/banksy-superhero-nurse-hospital-artwork/.

11 Tom Zytaruk, "Surrey Food Bank Boss Feezah Jaffer on Cheerios Box," *Surrey Now-Leader*, May 25, 2020, surreynowleader.com/news/surrey-food-bank-boss-feezah-jaffer-on-cheerios-box/.

12 Marcel Schwantes, "Want to Totally Transform Your Leadership? Give This to Your Employees Once Per Week," *Inc.*, November 22, 2016, inc.com/marcel-schwantes/research-says-this-absurdly-simple-habit-is-a-powerful-way-to-get-employees-moti.html; Melanie Curtin, "What Best Motivates You at Work? When 200,000 Employees Were Asked, This Was Their No. 1 Response," *Inc.*, March 31, 2018, inc.com/melanie-curtin/what-motivates-you-at-work-when-200000-workers-were-asked-this-was-their-top-reponse.html; Henna Inam,

"How Gratitude Can Help Us in Crisis," *Forbes*, March 12, 2020, forbes.com/sites/hennainam/2020/03/12/how-gratitude-can-help-us-in-crisis/.

13 Shankar Krishnamoorthy, "The Positive Power of Appreciation," SHRM, June 30, 2014, shrm.org/hr-today/news/hr-magazine/pages/the-positive-power-of-appreciation.aspx.

14 Jamie Thom, "Well Done? A Guide to Using Praise Effectively in the Classroom," *The Guardian*, October 18, 2017, theguardian.com/teacher-network/teacher-blog/2017/oct/18/well-done-a-guide-to-using-praise-effectively-in-the-classroom; Scott Halford, "5 Steps for Giving Productive Feedback," *Entrepreneur*, April 7, 2011, entrepreneur.com/article/219437; "The Skill of Praising," The Center for Parenting Education, accessed July 23, 2020, centerforparentingeducation.org/library-of-articles/healthy-communication/the-skill-of-praising/; Kristi Hedges, "How to Give Concise Positive Feedback," *Forbes*, October 7, 2015, forbes.com/sites/work-in-progress/2015/10/07/how-to-give-concise-positive-feedback/.

15 Rodger Dean Duncan, "How an Attitude of Gratitude Can Make You a Better Leader," *Forbes*, July 16, 2019, forbes.com/sites/rodgerdeanduncan/2019/07/16/how-an-attitude-of-gratitude-can-make-you-a-better-leader/.

16 "Giving Thanks Can Make You Happier," *Harvard HEALTHbeat*, accessed July 23, 2020, health.harvard.edu/healthbeat/giving-thanks-can-make-you-happier.

17 Jessica Stillman, "Gratitude Physically Changes Your Brain, New Study Says," *Inc.*, January 15, 2016, inc.com/jessica-stillman/the-amazing-way-gratitude-rewires-your-brain-for-happiness.html; Joel Wong and Joshua Brown, "How Gratitude Changes You and Your Brain," *Greater Good Magazine*, June 6, 2017, greatergood.berkeley.edu/article/item/how_gratitude_changes_you_and_your_brain; Jessica Stillman, "The Cure for Impatience: Gratitude," *Inc.*, April 7, 2014, inc.com/jessica-stillman/the-cure-for-impatience-gratitude.html; Christina Karns, "New Thoughts about Gratitude, Charity and Our Brains," *Washington Post*, December 23, 2018, washingtonpost.com/national/health-science/new-thoughts-about-gratitude-charity-and-our-brains/2018/12/21/238986e6-f808-11e8-8d64-4e79db33382f_story.html.

18 Jessica Stillman, "5 Ways Successful People Keep Calm," *Inc.*, August 19, 2014, inc.com/jessica-stillman/5-ways-successful-people-keep-calm.html; Alex Korb, "The Grateful Brain: The Neuroscience of Giving Thanks," *Psychology Today*, November 20, 2012, psychologytoday.com/us/blog/prefrontal-nudity/201211/the-grateful-brain.

19 Stillman, "Gratitude Physically Changes Your Brain."

20 "Hollywood Star Tom Cruise Spends Hours with UK Fans," BBC News, July 23, 2010, bbc.com/news/av/entertainment-arts-10736557; Alison Willmore, "Tom Cruise's Undying Hustle Is What Makes the 'Mission: Impossible' Movies So Good," *BuzzFeed News*, July 26, 2018, buzzfeednews.com/article/alisonwillmore/tom-cruise-stunts-mission-impossible-fallout.

21 F. Diane Barth, "Want to Be Famous? There's More to That Wish Than You Think," *Psychology Today*, January 15, 2011, psychologytoday.com/us/blog/the-couch/201101/want-be-famous-theres-more-wish-you-think.

22 Elizabeth Landau, "How the 'Fame Motive' Makes You Want to Be a Star,"
    CNN, October 28, 2009, cnn.com/2009/HEALTH/10/28/psychology.fame.
    celebrity/.

23 Jenny Anderson, "There Are Two Kinds of Popularity and We Are Choosing
    the Wrong One," *Quartz*, July 13, 2017, qz.com/1027802/there-are-two-kinds-
    of-popularity-and-we-are-choosing-the-wrong-one/.

24 "SC Featured: A Dog's Remarkable Journey to Find a Home," ESPN (video),
    13:54, March 3, 2017, espn.com/watch/player/_/id/18814225/lang/en/country/
    us. There's also a great book written by the man who adopted Arthur: Mikael
    Lindnord, *Arthur: The Dog Who Crossed the Jungle to Find a Home* (Vancouver,
    BC: Greystone Books, 2017).

25 David Ludden, "4 Reasons Why We Forget People's Names," *Psychology Today*,
    September 2, 2017, psychologytoday.com/ca/blog/talking-apes/201709/4-
    reasons-why-we-forget-peoples-names.

26 Helen Coster, "Top Tips: 10 Simple Tricks to Remembering Names,"
    Forbes, April 20, 2010, forbes.com/2010/04/20/how-to-remember-names-
    entrepreneurs-human-resources-remember-names_slide.html.

27 Katerina Georgieva, "Raptors' Nick Nurse Surprises Mississauga Music
    Teacher with $25K for New Instruments," CBC News, July 21, 2020, cbc.ca/
    news/canada/toronto/mississauga-music-teacher-gets-25k-new-instruments-
    1.5656584.

28 Peter Lane Taylor, "The Art of Giftology: How to Expand Your Business and
    Increase Sales through Gift Giving," *Forbes*, June 20, 2016, forbes.com/sites/
    petertaylor/2016/06/20/how-to-expand-your-business-and-increase-sales-
    through-the-art-of-giftology/.

29 "Restoring Dignity to Those on the Downtown Eastside," Citytv, YouTube
    (video), 4:18, August 20, 2015, youtube.com/watch?v=DOZvuO3s9vA; "I Get
    To," Whole Way House, accessed May 21, 2019, wholewayhouse.ca/i-get-to-
    legacy/.

30 Chip Heath and Dan Heath, *The Power of Moments: Why Certain Experiences
    Have Extraordinary Impact* (New York, NY: Simon & Schuster, 2017).

31 Jason Duaine Hahn, "Retired Kansas Farmer Who Mailed N95 Mask to Andrew
    Cuomo Is Awarded College Degree," *People*, May 6, 2020, people.com/human-
    interest/retired-farmer-who-gave-lone-n95-mask-to-new-york-earns-degree/.

32 Abdirahim Saeed, "Coronavirus: German Ikea Car Park Used for Mass Eid
    Prayer," BBC News, May 26, 2020, bbc.com/news/world-europe-52759511.

Connect in a Virtual World

1   Monica Torres, "Why Replying 'OK' in Work Chats Sounds So Aggressive,
    According to an Internet Linguist," *HuffPost*, February 13, 2019, huffingtonpost
    .ca/entry/okay-ok-k-workplace-language_l_5c619182e4b0910c63f35750.

2   Ryan Jenkins, "50 Percent of Emails and Texts Are Misunderstood, but There's
    an Easy Way to Change That," *Entrepreneur*, February 27, 2020, entrepreneur.
    com/article/346802.

3 Ibid.

4 Tom Warren, "Zoom Grows to 300 Million Meeting Participants Despite Security Backlash," *The Verge*, April 23, 2020, theverge.com/2020/4/23/ 21232401/zoom-300-million-users-growth-coronavirus-pandemic-security-privacy-concerns-response.

5 Libby Sander and Oliver Bauman, "Zoom Fatigue Is Real—Here's Why Video Calls Are So Draining," TED, May 19, 2020, ideas.ted.com/zoom-fatigue-is-real-heres-why-video-calls-are-so-draining/.

6 All quotations by Nick Morgan in this chapter have been taken from a personal interview with the author.

7 Kate Murphy, "Why Zoom Is Terrible," *New York Times*, April 29, 2020, nytimes.com/2020/04/29/sunday-review/zoom-video-conference.html.

8 Gianpiero Petriglieri (@gpetriglieri), Twitter post, April 3, 2020, 4:46 p.m., twitter.com/gpetriglieri/status/1246222551799541763?lang=en.

9 "Gartner CFO Survey Reveals 74% Intend to Shift Some Employees to Remote Work Permanently," Gartner, April 3, 2020, gartner.com/en/newsroom/press-releases/2020-04-03-gartner-cfo-surey-reveals-74-percent-of-organizations-to-shift-some-employees-to-remote-work-permanently2; "Cushman & Wakefield Research Predicts New Normal for Workplace," Business Wire, May 27, 2020, businesswire.com/news/home/20200527005640/en/ Cushman-Wakefield-Research-Predicts-New-Normal-Workplace.

10 Bryan Robinson, "What Studies Reveal about Social Distancing and Remote Working during Coronavirus," *Forbes*, April 4, 2020, forbes.com/sites/ bryanrobinson/2020/04/04/what-7-studies-show-about-social-distancing-and-remote-working-during-covid-19/.

11 Emilie Le Beau Lucchesi, "The Stresses of the Way We Work Now," *New York Times*, May 14, 2020, nytimes.com/2020/05/14/well/mind/coronavirus-work-stress-unemployment-depression-anxiety.html.

12 Garen Staglin, "When Home Becomes the Workplace: Mental Health and Remote Work," *Forbes*, March 17, 2020, forbes.com/sites/onemind/2020/ 03/17/when-home-becomes-the-workplace-mental-health-and-remote-work/.

13 Rani Molla, "Office Work Will Never Be the Same," *Vox*, May 21, 2020, vox. com/recode/2020/5/21/21234242/coronavirus-covid-19-remote-work-from-home-office-reopening.

14 Adedayo Akala, "More Big Employers Are Talking about Permanent Work-from-Home Positions," CNBC, May 1, 2020, cnbc.com/2020/05/01/ major-companies-talking-about-permanent-work-from-home-positions.html.

15 J. Stewart Black, "Laughter Will Keep Your Team Connected—Even While You're Apart," *Harvard Business Review*, May 27, 2020, hbr.org/2020/05/ laughter-will-keep-your-team-connected-even-while-youre-apart.

The Future Is Human

1 "History of 1918 Flu Pandemic," Centers for Disease Control and Prevention, March 21, 2018, cdc.gov/flu/pandemic-resources/1918-commemoration/1918-

pandemic-history.htm; "Influenza 1918," *The American Experience* (season 10, episode 10), PBS (documentary), 53:00, aired February 9, 1988, pbs.org/wgbh/ americanexperience/films/influenza/; Noah Y. Kim, "How the 1918 Pandemic Frayed Social Bonds," *The Atlantic*, March 31, 2020, theatlantic.com/family/ archive/2020/03/coronavirus-loneliness-and-mistrust-1918-flu-pandemic- quarantine/609163/.

2   Yascha Mounk, "Prepare for the Roaring Twenties," *The Atlantic*, May 21, 2020, theatlantic.com/ideas/archive/2020/05/i-predict-your-predictions-are-wrong/ 611896/; Kimberly Amadeo, "1920s Economy: What Made the Twenties Roar," *The Balance*, April 13, 2020, thebalance.com/roaring-twenties-4060511.

3   Yuval Noah Harari, "Yuval Noah Harari: The World after Coronavirus," *Financial Times*, March 19, 2020, ft.com/content/19d90308-6858-11ea-a3c9- 1fe6fedcca75.

4   Mounk, "Prepare for the Roaring Twenties."

5   "How Pandemics Change Society," *The Week*, May 24, 2020, theweek.com/ articles/915738/how-pandemics-change-society.

6   Ramona Schindelheim, "Yang: 'We're Experiencing 10 Years of Change in 10 Weeks,'" *WorkingNation*, April 28, 2020, workingnation.com/yang-were- experiencing-10-years-of-change-in-10-weeks/.

7   Chris Stokel-Walker, "How Personal Contact Will Change Post-Covid-19," BBC, April 29, 2020, bbc.com/future/article/20200429-will-personal-contact- change-due-to-coronavirus.

8   Jennifer Moss, "What Will Happen to Handshakes and Hugs after COVID?" CBC News, June 14, 2020, cbc.ca/news/canada/kitchener-waterloo/ jennifer-moss-happiness-column-handshakes-hugs-after-covid-1.5609465.

9   "Protect Your Brain from Stress," *Harvard HEALTHbeat*, August 2018, health. harvard.edu/mind-and-mood/protect-your-brain-from-stress.

10   Tracy Brower, "How to Focus on Your Work When All You Can Think about Is COVID-19: Five Simple Steps," *Forbes*, March 29, 2020, forbes.com/sites/ tracybrower/2020/03/29/how-to-focus-on-your-work-when-all-you-can-think- about-is-covid-19-five-simple-steps/.

11   Chris Ciolli, "Beyond the Handshake: How People Greet Each Other around the World," *AFAR*, April 8, 2020, afar.com/magazine/beyond-the-handshake- how-people-greet-each-other-around-the-world.

12   Jen Geller and Riley de León, "How Post-Pandemic Office Spaces Could Change Corporate Culture," CNBC, May 18, 2020, cnbc.com/2020/05/18/ how-post-pandemic-office-spaces-could-change-corporate-culture.html.

13   Radheyan Simonpillai, "Home for Good? Working Remotely Will Reshape Toronto's Office Culture," *NOW Magazine*, May 23, 2020, nowtoronto.com/ lifestyle/real-estate/work-from-home-reshape-toronto-office-culture/; Fred Bernstein, "How Architects Are Already Planning the Future of Offices," *Wall Street Journal*, May 22, 2020, wsj.com/articles/how-architects-are-already- planning-the-future-of-offices-11590152120.

14   "82% of Employees Expected to Return to the Office in 12–18 Months, Xerox Future of Work Survey Reveals," *Financial Post*, June 15, 2020,

financialpost.com/pmn/press-releases-pmn/business-wire-news-releases-pmn/82-of-employees-expected-to-return-to-the-office-in-12-18-months-xerox-future-of-work-survey-reveals.

15 Danny Crichton, "Work from Home Is Dead, Long Live Work from Anywhere," *TechCrunch*, May 18, 2020, techcrunch.com/2020/05/18/work-from-home-is-dead-long-live-work-from-anywhere/.

16 "Survey: How COVID-19 Is Changing the Workplace," SHRM, April 20, 2020, shrm.org/about-shrm/press-room/press-releases/pages/survey-how-covid-19-is-changing-the-workplace.aspx.

17 Clive Thompson, "What If Working from Home Goes On... Forever?" *New York Times*, June 9, 2020, nytimes.com/interactive/2020/06/09/magazine/remote-work-covid.html.

18 Brooke Simmons, "Selling in a COVID-19 World—4 Immediate Steps to Take," Outreach, July 16, 2020, outreach.io/blog/sell-in-a-covid-19-world.

19 Michael Owen, "How Fitness Will Change Forever," *The Atlantic*, May 29, 2020, theatlantic.com/health/archive/2020/05/how-pandemic-will-change-future-fitness/612187/.

20 Roger Lee, "What New Consumer Habits Will Stick Post-COVID-19? China Offers Clues," *Forbes*, May 19, 2020, forbes.com/sites/forbesfinancecouncil/2020/05/19/what-new-consumer-habits-will-stick-post-covid-19-china-offers-clues/.

21 "2020 CGS Customer Services Preferences in Times of Distress Survey," CGS, May 15, 2020, cgsinc.com/en/resources/customer-service-in-crisis; Shep Hyken, "Human Connection Is More Important Than Ever during Coronavirus," *Forbes*, May 17, 2020, forbes.com/sites/shephyken/2020/05/17/human-connection-is-more-important-than-ever-during-coronavirus/.

22 "Enjoy the Magic of Airbnb Experiences from the Comfort of Your Home," Airbnb, May 15, 2020, news.airbnb.com/enjoy-the-magic-of-airbnb-experiences-from-the-comfort-of-your-home/; Laura Begley Bloom, "How People Are Making Thousands by Hosting Virtual Airbnb Experiences (One Made $150k in a Month)," *Forbes*, May 22, 2020, forbes.com/sites/laurabegleybloom/2020/05/22/virtual-travel-airbnb-making-money/.

23 "Stay Adventurous: Bringing Abu Dhabi to You," Visit Abu Dhabi, accessed July 23, 2020, visitabudhabi.ae/stay-adventurous/explore.aspx.

24 Tim Ingham, "Why the Future of Livestreaming Isn't about Size or Popularity," *Rolling Stone*, May 29, 2020, rollingstone.com/pro/features/laura-marling-limited-livestreaming-1004936/.

25 Toyin Owoseje, "Keanu Wants to Go on a Zoom Date with You—For a Good Cause," CNN, June 17, 2020, cnn.com/2020/06/17/entertainment/keanu-reeves-zoom-auction-charity-intl-scli/index.html.

26 John Koetsier, "Virtual Events up 1000% since COVID-19, with 52,000 on Just One Platform," *Forbes*, May 27, 2020, forbes.com/sites/johnkoetsier/2020/05/27/virtual-events-up-1000-with-52000-on-just-one-platform/.

27 Jil McIntosh, "Start Your Engines: Toronto Will Host the World's First
    Drive-in Art Exhibit," *Driving*, June 4, 2020, driving.ca/ford/features/
    feature-story/start-your-engines-toronto-will-host-the-worlds-first-drive-in-
    art-exhibit.
28 Philip Rosedale, "Come Together, in High Fidelity," *High Fidelity Blog*, May
    21, 2020, highfidelity.com/blog/summer-2020-beta-release-come-together-in-
    high-fidelity.
29 Michael Ronen, "Can We Create Digital Intimacy in Times of Physical
    Distancing?" *Medium*, May 12, 2020, medium.com/@ronenmichael/
    can-we-create-digital-intimacy-in-times-of-physical-distancing-a7d5c754446c.
30 Jimmy Ris (@JimmyRis), Twitter post, April 13, 2020, 12:24 p.m., twitter.
    com/JimmyRis/status/1249780394460950534.
31 Eric Ravenscraft, "The Future of Movie Theaters Might Look a Lot Like an
    Apple Store," *Medium*, May 19, 2020, onezero.medium.com/the-future-of-
    movie-theaters-might-look-a-lot-like-an-apple-store-185c941d02a5.

ACKNOWLEDGMENTS

THIS BOOK EXISTS because of the support of several incredible people.

I have Dad to thank for many lessons, including this one in particular:

"Everything is temporary, but your potential is permanent."

He shared those words with me hours before I got married. His guidance over 40 years, along with his final lesson to "act now"—a lesson I truly realized after he suddenly left us—were huge motivating factors to finally write the book I've always talked about. Mom, I admire your strength and am grateful for the continuous love and encouragement both you and Dad have always given me.

Lori, my love and queen of quality control. Thank you for your patience, for your honest feedback, and for believing in your husband. This process was a marathon, yet you never stopped cheering me on to cross the finish line, especially during one of the toughest years of our lives. Your support made a world of difference.

Zain, thanks for pushing me to think bigger, get creative, and show up in dynamic ways. Your innovative mind consistently inspires me to strive to deliver the "wow" in any moment.

Nick, you are the magician that mapped our way through this wonderful maze. One optimistic email turned into our dinner conversation that changed my life. I have nothing but respect and gratitude for the endless feedback that you and Sarah provided on countless drafts. Thanks to you both for being terrific teachers and making the writing process such a rewarding experience.

Jesse, Chris, Peter, Caela, Alison, and the entire Page Two team, you have my utmost appreciation. You believed in the "Every Conversation Counts" message from the beginning. Your insight and extraordinary feedback helped make these pages a powerful resource to promote human connection.

To the guests who have allowed me to ask them personal questions over the years, thank you for trusting me with your story, your fears, and your message.

To my extended family, front line and the pandas, thank you for your unwavering belief in what this vision could be.

To you the reader who has made it this far, thank you for your attention and interest. I sincerely hope these ideas help you build the relationships you want to have in your life.

Curtis, thanks for contributing your wise words and for the continuous support from Sean and the Innovative Fitness team.

Finally, to Nico. My son, you really are the bringer of joy. While working on this book, I got to spend so many memorable days with you watching you smile, clap, and dance at home. I will never forget this special time we shared together. I hope you read this book one day and are inspired to go after your own dreams. I'm proud to be your "dada" and will always be a believer in your potential.

ABOUT THE AUTHOR

RIAZ MEGHJI is a human connection keynote speaker and an accomplished broadcaster with 17 years of television hosting experience; he has interviewed experts on current affairs, sports, entertainment, politics, and business. His on-camera experience not only taught him the power of a candid conversation, but also how to put it into practice.

Riaz has hosted for Citytv's *Breakfast Television*, MTV Canada, TEDxVancouver, CTV News, and the Toronto International Film Festival. He is a natural storyteller with a proven ability to conduct engaging, in-depth conversations across various disciplines.

Off camera, Riaz dedicates himself to philanthropy and causes he cares about including Canuck Place Children's Hospice and Covenant House. He holds a degree in business from Simon Fraser University and studied leadership communication at Harvard Extension School and the Canadian Management Centre. He lives in Vancouver, BC, with his wife and son.

To have Riaz Meghji speak to your organization about the five habits of human connection found in *Every Conversation Counts* or for additional (virtual) presentation training resources, please visit **RiazMeghji.com**.